The Self-Care Habit

The Self-Care Habit

The 4-Step Formula to Ditch the Stress and Find Your Flow

Aditi Ramchandani

Published by
Hybrid Global Publishing
333 E 14th Street, #3C
New York, NY 10003

Manufactured in the United States of America, or in the United Kingdom when distributed elsewhere.

Ramchandani, Aditi.
The Self-Care Habit
    ISBN: 978-1-957013-47-3
    eBook: 978-1-957013-48-0

Cover design by: Joe Potter
Developmental editing by: Claudia Volkman
Copyediting by: Dea Gunning
Interior design by: Suba Murugan

www.aditicreative.com

In loving memory of Kapil Bhaiya (1974–2020), who inspired me to follow my calling no matter what

Special Thanks

A shout-out to each person who preordered this book before it was written. I feel especially grateful for your support and belief in me. Thank you from the bottom of my heart. You helped make this book happen! Thank you to:

Kimeiko Rae Vision	Chaithra Reddy
Sweta Iyer	Ajay Maduskar
Nikki Green	Dawud Wallace
Danielle Bradley	Puja Patel
Dena Mansfield	Varun Arora
Ruth Goncalves	Aditi Ramchandani
Loretta Veney	Mosmi Shah
Rebecca Davis	Brian Hogan
Suzy Rosenstein	Jill Kempner
Kaulin Jani	Neetu Sabharwal
Manjesh Reddy	Dana Garced
Lydia Watson	Brian Canali
Lauren Ciesco	Judith Elliott
Sanjana Biswas	Karissa Knurowski
Amy Fuentes	Wendy Coop
Karen Astromsky	Florent D'Souza
Sonal Taneja	Lena Ransfer
Jocelyn Brady	Richa Mehta
Neetu Sachdeva	Ashley Evenson
Tina Pherwani	Ravi Jumani
Priya Patel	Raj Bhasin
Darwin Li	Dhruv Chhabra
Gail Gramlich	Anoop Kumar
Deb Childs	Jami Lee Avery

Sahil Ramchandani
Devi Patel
Deepal Patadia
Kim Guillory
Eva Leobold
Romola Breckenridge
Vijay Verma
Teresa George
Sabina Arora
Deepa Ramamurthi
Anita Ramchandani
Bikky Ramchandani
Anu Anand
Aarti Turuvekere

Emily Kavanagh
Janet Sprissler
Gretchen Hernandez
Evon Davis
Aditi Lowry
Vinod Asri
Madeline Klotz
Katy Calbreath
Eric Osterlind
Ayanshu Kumar
Lauryn King
Natalie Tellez
Ilya Perchikovsky
Afshin Virani

Contents

Introduction

As you start to walk on the way, the way appears.
Rumi

Self-care saved my life. It is the reason I am writing this book. During one of the lowest points in my life when I felt hopeless, defeated, and drained, self-care is what got me through. Whatever brought you to this book, I truly believe self-care will help you in any area of your life.

Pouring into yourself will always be a positive benefit. It's like eating nutritious food—it will always be beneficial to your optimal functioning. That's how I want you to think of self-care—a positive gain.

You might have found yourself reading this book because:
- You want to practice self-care but have no idea where to start.
- You're tired of being stressed and missing out on life.
- You're curious and want to add new tools to your belt.
- You're at your wit's end and your body is screaming for relief.
- You're surviving but know your current way isn't sustainable.
- You're ready to start *really* living and stress less.

No matter what led you here, you've come to the right place. My intention in writing this book is to give you the tools to navigate your own journey so you can live a life that is more than just a never-ending stress ball. To help bring the concepts to life, I've included real life examples, stories, and additional resources to take your self-care study further. You will also find activities to complete and writing prompts to journal and reflect on. In this journey together, we're going to turn your stress habits into self-care habits that nurture, motivate, and enliven you.

Building Your Self-Care Muscle

I've been extremely vulnerable to stress my whole life, especially as a highly sensitive person and an empath. I'm talking hair loss, pimples, getting sick, gaining weight, emotional meltdowns, and even a half-paralyzed face at age twenty (storytime on that later).

Years of chronic stress, depression, and burnout forced me to seek solutions when the physical and emotional burdens became too heavy to carry. If you're feeling this way too, know that you're not alone.

In one of my lowest moments, I reached a profound revelation that catapulted my self-care journey. I was lying in a bathtub for hours, crying and thinking I wasn't going to make it, and that's when it hit me: *No one was coming to save me.*

As I sunk deeper into the tub, feeling hopeless, a new thought arose: *Well, if I want to get out of this misery, I'm going to have to save myself.* For the first time in weeks, I saw a way out. It was an aha moment that opened up new possibilities for me. I was up for the challenge because I knew I couldn't stay in that tub forever. I accepted the assignment. I was going to save myself or die trying.

The first thing I decided to do was UP my self-care by 1,000 percent. I had no idea what that meant, but I thought it would be a good start. I put on my self-care cape and climbed out of that hole over the following months. I was shocked, because last time I had felt this way it took me over two years to climb out.

That moment in the bathtub is what birthed this book. I wondered, how many other people were in deep suffering like this and how were they making it through life? I told myself, "If I ever get to the other side of this, I must help others climb out of their hole too." I even brainstormed titles of the book while in the tub. It's funny to think about now. The first title of this book was something intense like *Shattered Glass* or *Broken Pieces*.

That experience is where my strongest self-care muscle was built. The lessons I learned, the tools I practiced, the level of care I took of myself was something I've been able to come back to often over the years. It's almost like that experience set the blueprint for the future. And really set the blueprint of this book.

You will be building your own self-care muscle as you read through this book. It will be your own blueprint that you can come back to, time and time again.

The Gifts of Pain

My cousin got certified to become a full-time meditation teacher. He told me he'd been wanting to do it for years but finally gained the courage to make the leap and leave the tech industry. Weeks before he was about to move to another country and embark on his new lease on life, he unexpectedly passed away.

This happened right when the 2020 COVID-19 pandemic hit. I felt devastated, just like many of us experienced in varying forms during this pandemic. It left me feeling hopeless and angry about life. I thought to myself, *What is the point of pursuing anything if you're going to drop dead right before it happens?* After contemplating and reflecting for months, I realized I had to do something because I couldn't live with this level of pain anymore.

That's when I participated in a 100-day self-care journey. I decided to focus on my mental, physical, and spiritual health. I was inspired by my friend who was doing a challenge called 75 HARD, created by Andy Frisella. The challenge sounded absolutely insane, including two workouts a day, drinking one gallon of water daily, and more. But what intrigued me about this challenge is that it's actually a mental toughness program rather than a fitness program.

I wanted mental toughness. So I created my own version of this program catered to my goals. This challenge was life-changing for me and opened up many doors. It did wonders for my mental health, confidence, and overall mood in life. I thought, *Okay, if I DID drop dead tomorrow, at least I did something pretty awesome for myself!* It made me feel proud of myself in a new way that I hadn't experienced in a while.

At the end of this book, you will be creating and completing your own 100-day self-care challenge. In just 100 days you can feel transformed from the inside out, which is pretty badass! If this sounds daunting to you, don't worry, I'm going to walk with you every step of the way.

The low points in our lives become catalysts for change in our life. How can you use these challenging moments to help you take care of yourself in a new way? Each of these low points allowed me to build a deeper relationship with myself and build new levels of resilience, patience, and love.

I wondered whether these same self-care tools I used during my hardest moments would work in my daily life. I started applying similar tools to burnout, stress, and overwhelm and found refreshing results. I started teaching them to my clients, and they experienced similar results.

To make it easier to plug-and-play in life, I created a stress management tool and self-care formula for myself and my clients. I wrote articles for publications like *Entrepreneur, Addicted2Success, Thrive Global, Good Men Project,* and more. People found the tips useful, and soon I was invited to deliver a stress management talk at a billion-dollar company during the pandemic. I was blown away at what was happening!

My Pain Truly Became a Gift and Led Me to My Purpose

As I started delivering talks, I realized there was no way I could give people everything they needed to know in sixty minutes. That's when I knew it was time to write a book. I thought, *Wouldn't it be great if they could have a manual with everything they need to start their self-care journey?*

This Book Is Dedicated to My Cousin

He passed away on my birthday and I felt it was a message for me: *Don't waste away in misery and go follow what calls you.* Because my cousin wasn't able to follow his calling and carry out his purpose, I feel even stronger that I must. I can smell his scent in the air near me as I'm writing these words. I can feel him nodding his head in joy that I am writing this book. Thank you, Bhaiya, for your help and blessings.

That experience made me think about the un-promised time we have. We could literally exit this planet tomorrow without warning. We are so blessed to have this opportunity to be in a human body in this time and space. How can we make the most of it? How can we live in alignment with our hearts?

How Can We Live a Less Stressed and More Meaningful Life?

I'm going to share with you tools to help kickstart and continue with that process.

Your Self-Care Journey Begins Now

One thing I learned from working with over two hundred clients in my coaching practice is that no one knows what self-care is. It's a buzzword that we all hear, but what is it exactly? And how do you do it? Most have no clue. I didn't either. We are going to discover what self-care is together.

I've divided this book into three parts: Foundations, Formula, and Flow. Though there is a wealth of information in this book, don't wait till the end to start. **Your self-care journey begins now.** As you read these pages, I want you to notice, observe, and think deeper about your life, the things around you, who you are, and what you desire. There is no need to worry about making changes just yet. Just observe yourself a bit more, and slowly you will start small practices and make small tweaks.

You can read the book from front to back or skip around to the sections you feel called to. There is no proper way to read this book. Though, if you ask me, I recommend starting with Part One so you can lead with intention and focus as you navigate your journey.

In this book you're going to:

- Learn a simple self-care formula to use for daily and long-term stress.
- Gain a greater understanding of what self-care is, what it looks like, and how to do it (for yourself).
- Build a personalized roadmap to ditch your stress habits and turn them into self-care habits.

Foundations

In Part One of the book, we are going to understand ourselves, understand self-care, and understand our current mindset. We are going to lay the groundwork for success and let go of parts that aren't working for us anymore. When we jump into something without any preparation or intention, it can make it harder to stick with for the long term. The work we do in the Foundations section will prepare us for a long-lasting self-care journey rather than something we just tried for ten days. At the end of this section, you will find a Self-Care QuickStart Guide so you can kick off your journey right away rather than wait until you finish the book.

Formula

In Part Two, you will learn the CARE formula to help you navigate short-term and long-term stress as well as guide you in creating a self-care practice. We will go over the formula and then dive into each of the four steps:

- Compassion
- Attention
- Recharge
- Engage

I have included steps you can follow, activities for you to practice, and real-life examples that will help bring the tools to life. You can do the exercises as you read the book or go back and do them after reading all of it. To gain results from this book, you need to actively engage the concepts and tools in your life—even if that means just 1 percent more engagement than yesterday.

Flow

In Part Three, we will talk about implementing these tools into your everyday life. We will cover special topics like:

- Burnout Recovery
- Work/Life Balance
- Depression
- Anxiety
- Habit Formation
- Building Your 100-Day Self-Care Road Map

I'm super excited for this section because this is where the magic happens. It's where you start to see the fruits of your efforts come to life. This is where self-care stops being a thing to do and evolves into something you become. This is where you get into the rhythm of self-care. This is where you find your flow.

A special note: In this book, I reference the terms God, Universe, Divine Intelligence, Soul, Cosmos interchangeably because it is a big part of my journey. If this doesn't resonate with you, feel free to ignore it or replace it with whatever you believe in: energy, matter, consciousness, atoms, creativity, brain, space, you—or nothing at all.

The tools in this book work regardless of your beliefs at large. Allow yourself to read with an open mind and open heart. Take what resonates and leave what doesn't. Most importantly, try anything you feel an internal nudge to try. And try it at least one to three times before dismissing it.

Some of the stories in this book have been modified to protect the privacy of the people involved, but the essential core of the stories has been kept to deliver the greater meaning behind them.

Birthing This Book to Life

This book was created with over nine years of coaching experience, working with more than two hundred clients in the marketing and mental health fields, tools from my studies as a Certified Life Coach from The Life Coach School, a Certified Health Coach from The Institute of Integrative Nutrition, and knowledge from my favorite books and teachers. I've worked with many mentors in my life, and I am grateful for their guidance in helping me become the woman I was too fearful to become for many years.

A shout-out to all the coaches I've ever worked with, to my Shaman with whom I worked for more than ten years, learning about energy and emotional intelligence, and to all my peers and the Master Coaches in my Master Coach Training program! In the resources section at the back of this book, I share other book recommendations, videos, a list of practitioners I recommend, as well as further programs I've developed for you to deepen your self-care journey.

Thank you to the seventy-plus people who believed in me and preordered this book a year before it was published and months before even one word was written. You are my OGs.

To all the people who cheered me on as I went through this writing process, including the last weekend writing marathon, your kind words, comments, messages, and emails really kept me going when I wanted to cry and quit.

The humblest of thanks go to the Divine Mother; thank you for loving me and believing in me when I couldn't. Thank you for challenging me and encouraging me to write this book, and for sharing your healing medicine with the world. This book is for you.

A special thanks to you who are reading this book right now. My hope is that this book will be a manual and personal guide you can refer back to many times over. Wherever you are in your journey, I trust you will find exactly what you need. Taking the first step by getting this book is already opening doors and guiding your next steps.

My desire for you is to live a life that is greater than stress. A life that you are proud of and that allows you to experience deep meaning and fulfillment. I truly believe self-care is the path there.

Stress isn't going anywhere, but we can learn how to dance with it. To dance with the energy of life.

I'm excited to take this journey with you. Let's go!

PART ONE

Foundations

CHAPTER 1

Why Self-Care?

We carry inside us the wonders we seek outside us.
Rumi

"Your eye isn't closing," she said, staring at me from across the kitchen table.

"What are you talking about?" I asked.

"Your eye is literally NOT closing," she said, leaning in closer. "Try closing your eyes right now." And I did.

"SOMETHING IS WRONG, ADITI. YOUR EYE IS NOT CLOSING!" she said in terror. I could feel my heart sinking into panic, but I was convinced she didn't know what she was talking about. My eyes felt just fine. I didn't feel any different.

Feeling confused, I thought that maybe I was just having an allergic reaction. I started antibiotics for a cold the night before. I figured I would deal with it tomorrow.

"We have to call campus emergency right now, and you have to go to the hospital," my friend said. *WHAT?* I freaked out. That was the last place I wanted to go because doctors and hospitals intimidate me. A visit there typically meant something was wrong.

Ten minutes later the GW Emergency Medical Response Group (EMeRG) arrived, and I was bombarded by three medical students asking me questions, checking my body, and conducting their procedure.

I was in shock and having a full-blown panic attack. I was uncomfortable, scared, and overwhelmed. What was going on? What was about to happen? *Please, I don't want to go to the hospital,* my mind was screaming.

The campus medical group took me to the emergency room, and I was in the hospital the entire night. At three in the morning, the doctor came back with the test results. **He told me I had Bell's Palsy and my face was half-paralyzed.** I could not believe the words that were coming out of his mouth.

"What? What do you mean my face is half-paralyzed?" He explained the right side of my face was affected and that I wouldn't be able to perform regular activities like drink from a cup, blink my eye, or smell from my nose for a couple of months.

"But how did this happen?" He shared that my cold virus likely mutated because of stress, causing Bell's Palsy. Stress? This happened because of stress? My mind was spinning.

I couldn't make sense of what he was saying. How could this be happening because of stress? Was I really that stressed? I was only twenty years old. I wanted to cry and turn back time so I could fix this. Did I need to sleep more? Did I need to chill out with my extracurriculars? What was it?

For the next six weeks, I had to wear an eye-patch on my right eye around campus. Can you imagine the social suicide I experienced? Everyone was like, "What happened . . . Did this happen at the club last night?"

Bell's Palsy stayed for about three months, but the impact it left on me will last forever. I never thought that something happening inside of me, such as stress, could blow up in my face like that. It was the first time I was introduced to the idea that *your internal environment affects your external body.*

Why You Should Care About Stress

If you've lived on this planet for a few years, you've likely experienced some form of stress in your life. Helpful stress that saves us from danger, but also prolonged chronic stress that leads to emotional or physical suffering.

People are more stressed now than ever before. The World Health Organization has called stress the epidemic of the twenty-first century. If you look around, you can probably see stress in people's eyes, moods, and bodies. One-third of the global population reported feeling stressed, worried, and angry, according to a 2019 Gallup study. Stress affects every part of our lives. It affects the way we think, the way we make decisions, and the way we show up in the world. It directly affects our personal results and happiness.

If stress affects us so greatly, then why did many of us never learn this important skill at home, school, or work?

Before I started doing self-care work, I ran a marketing business for six years. I worked with small business owners and helped them tell their brand's story through written and video formats. Their package included coaching sessions to discuss brand strategy and implementation, but funnily enough, 80 percent of our coaching sessions were focused on stress and life management.

It made me realize how much people are struggling and dragging themselves through their days. Whether they are unhappy, exhausted, sad, carrying emotional baggage for years, grieving, or simply feel lost inside, they are barely surviving and floating above water.

Here are some ways stress affects our health:

- Stress is making us sick. Seventy percent to 90 percent of doctor's visits are due to stress, according to WebMD.
- Stress is killing us. "Stress is linked to the six leading causes of death: heart disease, cancer, lung ailments, accidents, cirrhosis of the liver, and suicide" (from Psych Central).

In addition to killing our bodies, stress is also killing our spirits. We care more about work than we do about our well-being and happiness. I believe this is because we have been taught to favor success over health. In the hustle culture we live in, it's considered normal to overwork, to be busy, and to be drowning in life.

> *The Chinese word for busy is "heart-killing."*
> TARA BRACH

Can you imagine how much of a healthier and happier society we'd have from JUST learning how to manage and reduce stress?

We've been taught from a young age to "work hard to get far in life." Unfortunately, many of us are working hard and not getting very far at all. We are caught in a never-ending loop of stress and doing.

One of my clients, Matt, told me, "Aditi, I feel like I have been working so hard these last three years, but I'm not going anywhere. It's like I'm on a never-ending treadmill with no real destination. I keep telling myself, *I will think about the future once I get through this day,* but now years have gone by. I don't want to live like this anymore. I want to enjoy my life. I want to have purpose in my life."

My heart went out to this client. I wished I could wave a magic wand to help him, but this was the path he had to walk on his own. We created a daily activity for him to focus on enjoyment that he didn't have to earn. This was very difficult for him. He had trouble with the idea of pleasure unless he earned it.

At the same time, he explained to me that even when he earned it, he found himself charting out his next goal, and never truly enjoying his accomplishments. It was a self-created torture chamber. He knew this wasn't sustainable and that he was on his way to burnout if he didn't adopt a new way.

I was moved by his awareness and desire to live differently. He knew where he wanted to go and was willing to try different things, even if it felt silly. He wanted to break out of his stress cycle. He realized he was working hard, but for what exactly? His accomplishments were not fulfilling him like he had hoped they would.

If you relate to Matt's story, you are not alone in feeling this way. This is just one story that represents many. A number of my clients have shared with me similar ideas and say that their accomplishments just aren't fulfilling them. They are wondering why they are so busy and accomplished but not happy. More and more people are feeling the call to slow down and look deeper at what their heart wants, rather than what their mind tells them.

I believe we came here to *truly live*, not live in constant dread.

Therefore, we should care about stress, because it is robbing us of the experience of life, taking away our power, and leaving us exhausted. It is killing us in more ways than one. Giving your power away to stress can be like letting someone else drive your car. It's time to take that power back, and it starts by caring about the stress in your life.

How Stress Shows Up

Stress is a natural response in our body that alerts us to danger or threat. Stress is a signal to our brain that attention is needed. Stress is useful in many ways because it lets us know that there is a problem.

The origin of stress can show up for people in different ways. It can come from specific life events, daily occurrences, or your internal wiring (your natural response style).

Examples of life events include death of a loved one, divorce, loss of a job, financial obligations, moving to a new home, getting married, chronic illness, injury, and more.

Examples of daily occurrences include paying rent and other bills, managing a home, raising kids, family obligations, work, emotional struggles like depression, anxiety, anger, and more.

Examples of your internal wiring include your thoughts, having excessive worry because that's what you learned growing up, a trauma response to a situation, having low self-esteem because of past experiences causing you to go into a negative spiral with certain triggers, and more.

Where or how it comes matters less than how you engage with it. We will go over how to identify your specific stressors so you can get a better understanding of your personal landscape.

Stress can show up in our lives in so many ways. Here is a small list of how stress can affect you:

- Headaches
- Body pains
- Emotional pain
- Brain fog
- Loss of sleep
- Weight gain
- Ulcers
- Burnout
- Hair loss
- High blood pressure
- Irritability

If I haven't convinced you yet why you should care about stress, let's look at how it's affecting you personally. Reading in theory versus investigating your own life makes you an active participant in engaging with your personal stress.

Identify Your Stress Symptoms
Answer these two questions by making a list:

1. What kind of stress symptoms are you experiencing in your life? (Consider physical/mental/spiritual, etc.)
2. What do you feel this stress is keeping you from experiencing or having? (Consider experiences, opportunities, emotions, etc.)

If you are nodding or cringing as you are reading this list and answering these questions, know that this is a normal response. When you first become aware of something you weren't aware of before, it can be overwhelming, and sometimes even traumatic. But here's what I want you to know. You aren't doomed. In fact, it's just the beginning of a beautiful opportunity in front of you—an opportunity to shift your relationship with stress to build a new one with self-care.

This is where the magic happens. This IS the work of stress management and self-care. Awareness is a huge first step.

What I invite you to do as you do this exercise is to approach it with curiosity and compassion. Think of yourself like an investigator rather than a judge. We are not here to judge ourselves; we are here to observe and make small adjustments that feel personally aligned to you.

How Burnout Happens

Burnout has been categorized as a disease by the World Health Organization in the 11th Revision of the International Classification of Diseases (ICD-11). Here is how it is defined in ICD-11:

> Burn-out is a syndrome conceptualized as resulting from chronic workplace stress that has not been successfully managed. It is characterized by three dimensions: feelings of energy depletion or exhaustion; increased mental distance from one's job, or feelings of negativism or cynicism related to one's job; and reduced professional efficacy.

The two most important things to point out in this burnout definition are 1) that there is chronic stress and 2) that it is not managed well. This means that to prevent and recover from burnout, your stress needs to be managed better. Burnout happens when you are not paying attention to, or ignoring your own body's signals.

Why do we work so much and cause ourselves to experience chronic work stress? There are many layers to that including the work environment culture we are in, as well as our personal working habits. When it comes to personal habits, work can become an addiction. It can give us meaning, it can help us feel seen and heard, it can help us feel important, and it can also be the perfect escape from other areas of our life.

Work Habits

Riya buried herself into work for three years after going through a traumatic divorce. She was working sixty-plus-hour weeks to keep herself busy and to avoid thinking about it. The hurt was too painful to face, so work became her perfect escape. She came to work with me when she was ready to practice self-care and release her inner burdens.

Through self-reflection and discovery work she realized how much she was hiding in her life. She decided to be bold, step out of her comfort zone, and go on a trip abroad by herself. It was one of the scariest and best things she did for herself. It invigorated her and opened a whole new world of possibility in her mind. She is now working less, feeling more balanced, and already creating her next set of travel plans. It gave me so much joy to see her thriving.

Identifying Your Work Habits

Start to notice your own work habits and what you are getting out of work. When do you find yourself working past your limits? What do you think compels you to overwork? What inner void is work filling for you?

If you aren't "working" in the traditional sense but are a caretaker, stay-at-home parent, or something else, you can still apply this to your lifestyle. Modify and adjust any exercises to match your current situation.

The answers to the questions may come right away, but it may also take some time to show up. These are deep questions that might require some introspection before the true answer comes up. Most importantly, it all starts by asking. In Chapter 9 we talk about Burnout Recovery and Creating Work/Life Balance. You will also find more exercises and information to dig deeper.

Self-Care: The Solution to Stress

There are more and more studies cropping up that show self-care is a strong solution to stress reduction. A study released by Microsoft in 2021 shows that taking short breaks (a form of self-care) dramatically reduces stress. Seeing this study inspired me to start taking a lot more breaks during work, and it's made a huge difference in my energy and productivity levels.

Stress is a part of our life and isn't going anywhere. Instead of trying to get rid of it, we have to find a new way to relate to it. Transforming and understanding your relationship to stress is a key part of your self-care.

Many people pop a pill to ease the pain (including me at times), but this is only a temporary fix. For long-term stress management, you must dig deeper. Understand your stress, pay attention to your needs, and fuel yourself with care.

Consider this book your self-care manual but also a create-your-own-adventure map because we are all unique. My clients often compare their self-care journey to others, and I remind them that what nurtures them might exhaust someone else. Initially, you might follow all the steps in the exact order you learn them, but over time you will make this process yours. You will find what works for you. Allow yourself to consider this a guidebook, but with blank pages for you to fill in for yourself.

There are some self-care ideas or concepts you may not connect to, and that's okay. Go toward the concepts and tools you resonate with to prevent redundancy. And if you're not sure, then make a decision and choose something that feels doable and realistic for you. Keep reading to understand what self-care looks like and how you can incorporate it into your life. It's important to understand the bigger landscape before we dive into the CARE Formula in part two.

Why Self-Care Matters

Self-care is your ticket to freedom. It's your ticket to *you*. Your life. Your joy. It opens doors for you that you may never have thought were possible. This has happened for me in my own life in many ways, and it still amazes me.

When you choose self-care, self-care chooses you back.

It's like when you decide to do something in regard to self-care and the universe somehow moved mountains you didn't think possible to make it happen. It's bonkers! And it's amazing! Notice if you see this happen for you. And tell me about it! I love it when this happens!

Self-Care:
- **Gives you your life back.** The internal trap you might feel by your personal stressors can be mitigated through self-care. It is your path through the forest.
- **Reduces stress.** It prevents and recovers burnout. It calms down your nervous system. It helps you reconnect with what truly matters to you. It allows you to take your power back.
- **Helps you tap into your greatest potential**. It allows you to experience new parts of yourself that you may have never experienced. It creates a new strength and resilience in you that you can use again and again.
- **Creates more energy, happiness, time, and so more**.

How Self-Care Impacts Your Life

When I introduce the idea of self-care to working professionals, they tell me they don't have time for it. And I totally get it. When you have a busy schedule and packed days, the last thing you want to think about is doing yet "another thing." That's why I want to propose a different idea to you.

What If Self-Care Was Less about "Doing" and More about "Being"?

A lot of my clients get caught up in the idea of "doing" self-care. "OMG, I didn't have time to go to yoga this week" or "I totally ate junk food on Saturday; I didn't eat clean like I planned," they'll tell me.

Here's where I want to invite you to shift your idea to what really matters. Self-care is not a list of duties to complete. It is about the person you are being to yourself.

Are you someone you can rely on for yourself? Are you someone who will have your own back when you are struggling? Are you someone who will listen to your personal struggles and hold space for yourself?

When you make this internal shift from doing to being, it's less about having time for it, but more about the way you are showing up in the world with the time you do have.

This is something you'll have to remind yourself of often. I have to remind myself of this all the time. Like I said, this manual is for me just as much as it is for you.

As you "become a self-care person" through the way that you think about it and about yourself, the actions will naturally come. You will want to go out for a walk because you know it'll help clear your head. You will want to eat greens because you feel how it fuels you. You will want to stretch because it helps you unwind from the day.

As you manage your stress and practice self-care, it will impact your life in beautiful ways. Instead of self-care "taking away from you," it will add to you.

Self-care fills up your cup. And when you pour into yourself, you will be able to pour that much into all areas of your life. It is filling up your tank so you can drive your car.

Here's a glimpse of all the benefits you'll get from managing stress:

- More energy
- More time
- Happiness
- Focus
- Better sleep
- Productivity
- Mental clarity
- Weight loss

- Weight maintenance
- Greater meaning
- Purpose
- Connection
- Joy
- Efficiency
- Innovation
- Resilience

- Health
- Creativity
- Emotional freedom
- Healing and repair

- More brain power
- Deeper peace
- Creative problem solving

Now that you know how self-care will add to your life. Let's create your own personal self-care intention to kick off your journey.

Your Self-Care Intention

You now have a general understanding of why stress matters, how it's affecting you, and what to do about it (self-care). It's time to personalize this journey for you.

Journal and Reflection Questions

1. Why does self-care matter to you?
2. What will self-care allow you to do?
3. Why do you want to practice self-care now vs later?

Use the answers to these questions to create your own self-care intention.

My self-care intention is:

_____

_____

_____

_____

_____

Before I share some examples with you, I want you to brainstorm from your own creative mind. Sometimes examples can limit us, and we only think of ideas within those constraints. So, think about what you want to get out of self-care and what your desire is before you read the examples below. Then you can use your ideas plus the examples below to fuel your own aligned intention.

Self-Care Intention Examples

- My intention with self-care is to have greater focus, deeper productivity, and space to enjoy my life more.
- My intention with self-care is to have a stronger body so I can keep up with my kids and go on more adventures with my family.
- My intention with self-care is to have more energy so I can keep up with the demands of work and home life.
- My intention with self-care is to live more.
- My intention with self-care is to have greater intimacy with myself and my relationships.
- My self-care intention is to feel good in my body so I can feel my best in any situation.
- My self-care intention is to love myself more.

Journal and Reflection Questions

1. How connected do you feel with your intention from 1-10 (10 being very connected)? What would make it a 10?
2. What emotions does it bring up for you?
3. What hindrances could stop you from self-care? How will you handle it when they do come up?

Feeling connected to your intention is crucial on this journey. It's easy for it to become another to-do, which will leave it sitting on the backburner. So, I highly encourage you to sit with your intention, for at least a few days. Truly connect to it and feel it in your entire being. Activate that intention within yourself. You can write it and post it somewhere, make it your password, or your phone background!

Now that you have your self-care intention, let's dive into building your self-care foundation!

CHAPTER 2

Building Your Self-Care Foundation

Follow your bliss and the universe will open doors for you, where there were only walls.
JOSEPH CAMPBELL

Have you noticed some of the most painful moments of your life are what made you stronger than ever? Some of the experiences I've had taught me that I can rely on myself, I have my own back, and I can get through tough moments. Having gone through those experiences built a strong foundation inside of me that I come back to often and keep on developing. I remind myself what I've done before and what I'm capable of, and I expand my mind into possibility.

We all have a foundation from which we are operating. It's one that was likely created many years ago, probably when we were children to our teen years. Up until now, that foundation has been our operating system. And how you do one thing is how you do everything. This means that the way you approach self-care will affect the results you get. I want you to get the most optimal results that you can for yourself, and in order to create new habits we are going to have to shake that foundation up. We are going to start at the bottom, destroy what's no longer working, and build from the bottom up. If you're scared, don't worry—as you experience the benefits, you'll shortly be wondering why you didn't do this sooner!

In this chapter, you are going to examine your current foundation and create a new layer that includes self-care. We are going to look at your personal self-care beliefs, the skills you need to practice self-care, and some helpful mindset tools to strengthen your journey. Building this foundation will allow for a greater self-care practice because it will help program your brain to choose self-care first rather than last. With a strong inner core, you can become your own greatest resource, you can set boundaries from a place of empowerment, and you can stand tall in a sea of people who believe differently than you. This will happen through intention, practice, and repetition.

Going Deeper Than Surface-Level Self-Care

When people think of self-care, they often envision spas and massages. But self-care goes so much deeper than that. That is just a surface level idea of self-care fed to us by the marketing industry that wants us to spend money.

Self-care touches so many dimensions—your mental, physical, and spiritual self. Most of us are familiar with the idea of diet and exercise because it's constantly being shown to us in ads, but this is just a small fraction of physical self-care. As you go through this book, you will discover what mental, physical, and spiritual needs you have as you do your own personal discovery work.

Another big proponent of self-care is building a partnership with you, yourself, and you. You are building a foundation of trust, love, and deep friendship with yourself. How can you treat yourself the way you would treat a friend? How can you care for yourself the way you would care for a loved one?

The friendship you build with yourself surpasses any other relationship you will have in your life. You are the only person you'll be with for your entire life. How can you make that relationship count? How can you make it special? You may not know all the answers to these questions right now, but asking them is what opens the doors for you to find those answers. Building a partnership with yourself is where the strength of your self-care embodiment lives.

Meet Yourself Where You Are

You are going to overbook yourself. You are going to be tired. You are going to wish you had said "no." You are going to be mad at yourself for not catching something sooner. But ultimately there's nothing you can do to change the past now.

Therefore, no matter what's going on in the moment, meet yourself where you are. That is the best form of self-care you can provide yourself. Be present with yourself in this moment rather than wishing or hoping to be elsewhere.

There were many times this past year that I got so angry at myself when I found myself getting sick or burned out. I would beat myself up about getting sick, which would only cause more self-torture, and this was the opposite of self-care.

So I just want to remind you that it's OKAY if you experienced burnout. It's OKAY if you got sick. You are not a bad person. You are not irresponsible. You could not have done this differently. Because if you could have, you would have. Give yourself grace. What you can do is *care for yourself now*. That's what matters most.

Find Your Own Rhythm

Your self-care is going to look different than the person next to you. The way you recharge might seem absolutely ridiculous to someone else and vice versa.

For some, cooking is the ultimate relaxation, while for others it's the most stressful thing possible. Some find it relaxing to be around people, while others prefer alone time. The point of the exploration process as you go through this book is to find what resonates with you.

Allow yourself to be inspired by others, but don't go into a comparison phase to the point that it blocks you from uncovering your authentic needs. This is where the self-discovery work comes in. You get to experience and discover who you are, what recharges you, and what fills up your cup. It's a beautiful journey of meeting yourself.

There's No Right or Wrong

We're often taught from a young age that there is a "right and wrong," a "good and bad." As adults we spend so much time evaluating whether we are doing something right that we miss the whole opportunity in front of us! This criteria is obsolete because what may be someone's right may be someone else's wrong and vice versa.

When it comes to self-care, there is no right or wrong. There is only what is right for you. And that is something only you can discover for yourself. No one will be able to know what's best for you or be able to decide that for you except you.

This is one of the most important foundations to lay inside your brain. As you go on this self-care journey, notice when you are going into this place in your mind. When you find yourself asking, "Am I doing this right?" instead ask yourself, "Is this right for me?" That is a more useful and productive question. Another great one is "If no one were watching, how would I care for myself right now?" This helps you disconnect from those constructs.

The Process Is Not Linear

I have written this book in a format that you can digest. It is linear on paper, but in real life it is not. You may have seen the graphic that shows what people think the path to success is (a straight line) and what it actually looks like (a big squiggly doodle that goes up and down and back and forth). Your self-care journey is similar. I often find my clients getting upset when they see an old pattern or habit pop back up. They feel like they have regressed, and all their work went to waste. But this is not true.

Every step you take toward self-care adds to your self-care bank. Just because something didn't go the way you planned, perhaps you didn't honor your time/energy the way you hoped to have, and maybe a trigger sent you into a negative spiral—this does not mean you've gone backward!

Life is full of unexpected turns, and instead of thinking that it's taking you backward, think of it as an opportunity to step into a whole new space. Or as an opportunity to see how far you've come.

This happened to me while writing this book. I was attending a gathering where I knew certain people would also be. I thought seeing them would trigger me into a negative spiral as it had in the past. Before the event, I experienced massive anxiety and a mini panic attack. But to my surprise, it ended up being quite a pleasant evening. I realized that this no longer had a hold on me, and that I had grown more than I thought.

Sometimes you have to come face-to-face with an old trauma to realize it no longer has a hold on you.

"New Level, Old Devil"

This is something I learned from Denise Duffield Thomas, author of *Get Rich, Lucky Bitch* and *The Chillpreneur*. She talks about money ceilings that come up every time you make a new breakthrough. When we are faced with a familiar emotion or trigger, that is the "old devil" that has reappeared, but now you are breaking through a "new level." It's not the same as before, and you are certainly not going backward. I always remind myself of this when I am breaking through a new layer in my life.

There are times when I was presented with an opportunity that—although it felt like hell—I used the new tools I had gained, and it was powerful to see the result change. Because I reacted differently, I got a different result. And that in itself is beautiful growth to see. Even though I had the same old trigger come up, I faced it differently, and that's what placed me into a whole new evolution of myself. Sometimes these old devils pop up so you can put your newfound tools and insights into practice and see how far you've grown!

Vision and Reflection Exercise

Now that we have the basics down, let's start the discovery process. As a reminder, self-care is less about what you are "doing" and more about who you are "being." So let's reflect on who you are and discover who you want to be. Use the questions below to explore what that looks like for you.

Journal and Reflection Questions

1. Reflection: Who am I being to myself currently?
2. Envision: Who do I want to be to myself?
3. Reflection: How do I currently care for myself?
4. Envision: What do I envision caring for myself to look like?
5. Reflection: In what ways do I currently care for myself like I would a friend?
6. Envision: How would I care for a friend in need? How can I do that for myself?
7. Reflection: What current values do I live by? What do I currently give importance to?
8. Envision: What do I value? What is important to me? What values do I want to live by?

9. Reflection: Why is self-care important to me? Why am I committed to it?

10. Envision: What will self-care do for me and allow me to do?

Answering these questions will help you create a strength inside of you because you will have a clear understanding on how you want to care for yourself. Most people have no idea, so they have nothing to base their decisions upon. You will know your needs, how to care for yourself, and have the tools to make it happen. Feel free to answer all the reflection questions first, and then all the envision questions next, or answer them in the way they are listed. See what works better for your brain to imagine. Then take the answers that are most relevant to create your "Self-Care Core." You can create a separate sheet (or page) that has *Self-Care Core* written at the top. Then write in the envisioned answers to these questions:

My Self-Care Core

- How do I treat myself?
- How do I care for myself?
- I care for myself like I do for a friend by:
- I value:
- What's important to me?
- I'm committed to self-care because . . .

By writing your self-care core, you are making a decision on how you will care for yourself. Now you will create space and take action on it. If this is hard for you to envision, below is an example of a Self-Care Core. You'll notice I go back and forth between the first and third person. This is because a mix of both helps me feel connected to myself as well as feel like I am being cared for from the outside. It's like I am my own inside and outside friend. Do what works for you. Whichever voice resonates best with you. This is a basic example, so allow yours to be as grandiose and verbose as you desire!

Sample Self-Care Core

How I treat myself:

- I listen to myself, I am kind to myself, I ask myself how I'm doing. I am someone who never leaves her side. I am someone who checks in on her. (Play with using the first and thirdrd person to relate to yourself in different ways.)

How I care for myself:

- By having deep compassion for myself. Listening. Giving her a hug. Honoring her desires. Honoring wherever I am in the moment, even if I don't like it. Hold her in pain. Be there for myself when I'm struggling, rather than abandoning her. I always have her back.

I care for myself like I do for a friend by:

- Not judging her. Having whole compassion for her. Listening intently. Holding her hand. Comforting her. Letting her vent. Holding space for her emotions.

I value:

- Experiences. Color. Alone time. Beauty. Deep conversations. Connection. Nature.

What's important to me:

- Space. Comfort. Freedom to be myself and do what I want. Relationships with like-minded people. Spending time outside.

I'm committed to self-care because:

- It makes me happy. It makes me feel better. I have more energy to do the things I want.

Make sure your commitment is in present tense rather than future tense. For example, instead of "I will have more energy," say "I have more energy." This plants the seed in your brain that it is already happening, and it will allow you to embody that self-care mode now.

A New Lens

Many people want to practice self-care, but they don't. This would often stump me. I would see that they had the means and resources to practice self-care, but why didn't they? I realized it's because of the place they are currently operating from.

Learning how to care for yourself requires you to have a new lens.

Sometimes I think of myself in third person to detach from my default view and to see myself from another perspective. If you were caring for a sick loved one, patient, client, or grieving friend, how would you take care of them?

In order to create a new lens, you have to start with understanding your current lens and then consciously create a new or polished lens that supports your wholeness. Ponder on how you view yourself now. Notice where you might tend to put yourself last, work past your limits, and not take a break because of guilt or avoidance.

As you notice these things, it will give you a lot of information about yourself. Some of this might be uncomfortable to view. For example, you might discover that you are overworking to avoid the pain/void/grief you feel inside. It may feel painful to face the truth. It's important to love yourself as you go through this process. And remember that facing the stress or pain will also help you release it. Facing the truth is self-care. It is the microscopic lens to the areas that require deeper care because it shines a light on where you are struggling.

Journal and Reflection Questions

1. How do I view myself?
2. How do I care for myself now?
3. How do I care for a friend or loved one?
4. Do I put myself first? Or Last? How so? Why?
5. Is there something/someone I care for more than myself? Why?
6. Do I work past my limits? Why? When? How?
7. Do I want to put myself first? Why or why not?
8. Do I feel guilty putting myself first? How is this impacting my health?
9. How do I want to view myself?
10. How would I like to care for myself?
11. What is the self-care lens I want to create for myself?
12. How would this new lens help me?

Your Self-Care Mindset

How you think about self-care is how you will show up in your self-care practice. If you believe self-care is selfish, that it requires a lot of money, or that it takes up too much time, that's exactly how you will show up in your self-care toward yourself.

So let's investigate your self-care beliefs. Write down everything you think about self-care. And let yourself get nasty with it—let any and every thought come up, even if you feel bad saying it. For example:

- Self-care is for losers.
- Self-care is for rich people.
- Self-care is for people who have too much free time.
- Self-care is for people who are selfish.
- Self-care is too hard.

Write down twenty or more ideas that you have about self-care. Don't think too hard; just let it free flow. Even if you only believe it 1 percent, write it down.

Now ask yourself, "What do I need to believe in order to allow self-care into my life?"

You might say things like:

- Self-care is for everyone, including me.
- Self-care doesn't have to take a lot of time.
- Self-care doesn't have to be expensive.
- Self-care is doable.

Here are some self-care beliefs that I recommend you start to instill in yourself:

- I deserve self-care.
- Self-care can be simple.
- Self-care isn't selfish, it's nutritious. It fills up my gas tank so I can drive.
- Self-care is free.
- Self-care can take as little as five minutes.
- Small breaks equal big results.
- Self-care allows me to have mental clarity and space for what matters.
- Self-care allows me to be a better me.
- Self-care is possible for me.
- Self-care helps me profoundly.

How do you instill new beliefs into yourself? Through repetition. Every time you find yourself with an old self-care belief, catch it, and remind yourself of your new truth. To help it stick, you need to create and find evidence to support it. As you continue to practice your new truth, it will become truth for you, and over time your old belief will phase out as the new one takes over.

A Common Care Blocker: Self-Care Is Selfish

Let's talk about this one because it comes up a lot. This statement doesn't have to mean that self-care is bad. Being selfish is actually a good thing. I listened to an audio recently from Abraham-Hicks, a teacher of consciousness, where they spoke about the idea of how we should absolutely be selfish:

> Being selfish means we are focusing on ourselves and on pleasing ourselves. And why shouldn't we? When people get mad at us for being selfish, are they implying we should instead be focusing on pleasing them? Now isn't that selfish?

That made me think about being selfish in a whole new way. Of course, we should be focused on us, or who else will?

When we are depleted, people pleasing, and living off-balanced lives, it serves no one. When we serve ourselves, we serve everybody. When we focus on ourselves, we make way to give and contribute in a impactful way.

Here are a few more helpful reminders to fuel your self-care mindset for success:

- This is not a race. My pace is perfectly perfect for me.
- My self-care is unique to me.
- Patience wins—some habits take three months to build, some three years. All of it is wonderful.
- One percent done is better than none. Small steps lead to big opportunities.

The Skills You Need to Practice Self-Care

Here's the inconvenient truth: The average person doesn't practice self-care. My hope is that this will change in the future as each person takes responsibility for and values their well-being. But for now, it may require you to be an outlier, at least temporarily, until you meet others with similar values. This is why to truly practice stress management it requires you to go against the grain.

Because stress is so normalized, it requires a certain skill set to manage it. You will see your peers overworking, over-planning, and being utterly exhausted. If you don't want to follow that same path, this is an invitation to make a different decision than your peers.

It might even take you to a place where people roll their eyes at you. This happens to me even today. Even though I TEACH self-care and stress management, there are still people who mock me when I PRACTICE self-care.

Do they not realize I teach this? Who would I be if I didn't practice what I teach?

It truly boggles my mind that people have so many opinions when you choose to care for yourself. If you encounter this on your journey, here's what I want you to know: Other people's comments have nothing to do with you. These people are triggered because they are not doing the same for themselves, and they are resentful and unconsciously envious.

They may say, "Who do you think you are to do this?" But really, they haven't given themselves the grace and permission to do the same for themselves. So instead, they may call you selfish, lazy, or spoiled. This is why this skillset is SO important to help you navigate all the different situations you may encounter.

Four Skills to Cultivate

Courage: This bravery will allow you to have difficult conversations and build boundaries to create the self-care practice that nurtures you. This is also going to help you through any resistance or discomfort you feel in building new practices.

Confidence: Having a strong sense of self will allow you to make decisions that are right for you, no matter what anyone has to say about it.

Introspection: This skill will allow you to dig deeper and understand your own habits, and limitations, process emotions, and to explore all the possibilities that are available to you. This will serve you well in creating solutions that you've never thought of before.

Execution: This skill will allow you to implement what you are learning in your life rather than just thinking about it.

These four skills will carry you through the social pressures, personal resistance, and discomfort you may experience as you practice self-care. Anytime you feel stuck, come back here and grab one of these skills to assist you in moving forward.

For example, I had a colleague who was struggling to create boundaries around her days off. She wanted to take time off but was getting notices from her manager to complete certain tasks. She told me her brain was mush, and she could barely get her work done.

In this case, she needed courage and confidence to do what was right for her, and to take care of the tasks once she was rested. She decided to speak to other colleagues to determine the urgency of the work, made a plan for when she'd complete the tasks on her next working day, and logged off for the remainder of her days off.

Once she understood the requirements and made a plan, she was able to completely logout on her days off and still complete all her work in time. It required bravery on her part to share her struggles with others, introspection to realize she needed space before she could finish, and the confidence to make a decision that worked for her and the execution to speak to the company about her needs.

Whenever you find yourself struggling to implement a self-care practice, come back to these skills and see which one might help. Often one of these skills will propel you to your next step.

Your Self-Care Is Your Responsibility

If you're waiting for a break from life, know that it's never going to happen unless you create that break yourself. No one is going to remind you to take care of yourself. No one is going to tell you it's time to put the devices down. No one is going to tell you it's time to take a break. Because people around you are likely not doing it either!

Therefore, it's important to remember that it's your job to take care of yourself. It's your job to fill up your own cup. The next time you find yourself feeling resentful because you are tired, burned out, and exhausted, ask yourself where your cup is feeling depleted and nurture that part of you. Do not rely on someone else or something else to fill that void. This is the greatest mistake we can make. To put our needs in someone else's hands is a sure way to have them not get met. Depending on others is a lose-lose battle.

No one can take care of you like you can because no one knows your specific needs like you do. That's why it's important to take responsibility for it. So, from now on, you are taking your self-care into your own hands. *Capeesh?*

The 1 Percent Win

One of the things I worried about in writing this book and in doing this work is people catching me in a stressful moment in real life. I feared they'd wonder, *THIS woman teaches stress management? How?*

Especially when there is an event, or guests coming over, or I am traveling or speaking, you may find me in a corner, losing my marbles.

I am a student of self-care just like you are. I'm not perfect, I don't have it all figured out, and at the same time I am way far ahead from where I was just five years ago. This manual is for me just as much as it is for you. My struggles with stress are exactly what have birthed this book. It has been my path to finding solutions.

I'm going to remind you of what I always remind my clients: Even doing just 1 percent of self-care (a tiny bit more than your usual) can go a long way. If you do just 1 percent of what is written in this book, that is INCREDIBLE. Over time you'll add another 1 percent, and another 1 percent. Allow yourself to take bits and pieces and apply small incremental changes and shifts. Reward yourself for it!

On the other hand, if you are one of those people who can go from 1 percent to 100 percent, meaning you can take big leaps and make big changes fast, then by all means go for it. Wherever you are, go at your own pace. You may have to discipline yourself more than others at times. This is not a race. You don't have to figure this all out in one month, or even six months. It may be a slow, gradual process for some, and it may be an accelerated one for others. This has been a multi-year process for me, and it still continues. Allow yourself to be a student of self-care and don't judge your process. Honor yourself. And honor your pace.

The strong woman you see now
Was inside me all along
I just finally gave her permission to breathe
And be free
Of the chains and prisons in her mind
That kept her doubting and falling behind
ADITI RAMCHANDANI

CHAPTER 3

Self-Care QuickStart Guide

*The meaning of life is just to be alive. It is so plain and so obvious and
so simple. And yet, everybody rushes around in a great panic as if it were
necessary to achieve something beyond themselves.*
ALAN WATTS

Driving home from lunch, I noticed I felt a little loopy. I paused and
thought back over the last two hours. Did I have a drink (with alcohol)
at the restaurant? Hmm . . . no, I hadn't. So why did I feel this way?

I realized that I enjoyed my lunch with a childhood friend so much
that I felt high from it! It was one of those friendships that even if you
hadn't talked in months, you could pick right back up where you left
off. I felt energized after hanging out with her and realized that I was
high on life!

It reminded me about the importance of engaging activities that
nurture your soul and spirit. And I realized how much that was lacking
in my life. Because of that, I've started to add more time toward doing
more of what makes me feel alive.

This is your first tip to kickstart your self-care journey now!

Pursue Aliveness

How can you spend more time doing things that enliven you?

I wrote this QuickStart chapter so that you don't have to wait to read the whole book to start your self-care practice. I know there are a few of you that are like, "I don't have time to read a whole book; I need self-care NOW." If that's you, I got you in this chapter. But on the other hand, as they say, if you don't have time to meditate, then you need to meditate even more! So, in the same way, if you feel you don't have time for self-care, then this book is a must-read. As you jumpstart your journey with this chapter, I recommend you continue reading the book in order to learn and practice creating long-lasting self-care habits. Reading ten pages a day can go a long way!

Five Simple Ways to Up Your Self-Care

This is for the people who say, "Just tell me what to do." Here are my top five tips to up your self-care right away. Whenever I find myself wanting to up my self-care, I always start with these steps to get me going. These steps will nurture, cleanse, and reset you. If you do nothing but these five things, you'll already be boosting your internal and external health.

1. **Drink water**. Most of us can benefit from drinking more water. Our bodies function better. According to Harvard Health, water brings nutrients and oxygen to cells, aids digestion, flushes bacteria, and so much more. They recommend a four to six cup intake of water a day. For your personal intake, consult with a professional.

2. **Move**. Our bodies hold on to a lot of stress. They need an outlet to let some of that tension flow through and out. It can be as simple as stretching or walking for five minutes or more.

3. **Go outside**. Nature harmonizes and balances us. Simply spending ten minutes gazing into nature can be therapeutic and regulate your nervous system. It can relax and rejuvenate you.

Japanese researchers discovered that "forest bathing," essentially taking in the atmosphere of the nature, has benefits such as reducing blood pressure, improving moods, reducing stress, and more.

4. **Declutter and disconnect.** We hold on to a lot of things we don't need. This is your sign to Marie Kondo your life: let go of anything that doesn't bring you joy and keep what does. Cleaning up your physical space will clear your mental space. Take a break from digital devices. Leave your phone in another room for one hour, one day, or longer. It will feel awful at first because we are addicted to screens, but eventually you will feel amazing.

5. **Pursue aliveness.** Go do something that lights up your soul, is out of your comfort zone, or that is unfamiliar. You may have no clue what that means for you; that's what the discovery process is for. Notice over the next week what makes you feel alive. It could be spending time with certain people, going to certain places, or simply enjoying something in your home that you've neglected out of busyness.

In Chapter 7: Recharge, you will find additional ideas to rejuvenate. But for now you have a few simple steps to kickstart your self-care journey right now. You don't have to wait until the end to start.

Three Main Principles

We are going to look at three main areas: time, energy, and space.

The way you manage your time, energy, and space all impact your stress levels. This is something you can start to focus on right away by asking questions and observing how you live currently.

Three Main Principles

1. Time: Spend your time in a way that matters to you.
2. Energy: Manage and recharge your energy daily.
3. Space: Create space within and around yourself.

We will look at how you manage and spend your time, energy, and space in this section.

Journal and Reflection Questions

1. How do I spend my time each day? (Break it down hour by hour.)
2. What are my energy levels like on a daily basis?
3. What time of the day do I have the most energy? The least energy?
4. How do I recharge myself now?
5. What recharges my energy?
6. How is the space I am living in?
7. How is the space I am working in?
8. What's working and not working?
9. What is my mental space like?
10. How do I want to spend my time?
11. How do I want to manage my energy?
12. What do I wish I could do with my time?
13. What do I wish I could do with my energy?
14. How can I recharge myself going forward?
15. What kind of space do I want to live in? Work in? Drive in?
16. How can I create a nourishing space for me?
17. What kind of mental space do I want to have or be in?

The questions you want to continually ask yourself are:
- How can I spend my time in a way that matters to me?

- How can I manage my energy and recharge myself?
- How can I create space within and around myself?

Managing Your Energy

There are two parts to managing your energy: 1) paying attention to your energy expenditure (how you use your energy) and 2) noticing the way you charge yourself up (how you gain energy). Below is a wonderful way to help you think about this.

> Imagine that you have twenty-five marbles of energy a day. Each marble represents a token of energy you have. You might find that running in the morning actually gives you two extra marbles, but it also might use up one marble. You might find that visiting your relatives' house drains your energy by five marbles, but going to your best friend's house gives you three extra marbles of energy.

This is a great exercise to help you manage and realize how much energy you are using up in the day, how much you have left, and knowing when you need to recharge. For example: when you have no marbles left, your energy for the day is gone, and it's time to rest and not commit to anything else.

As someone who has major FOMO (Fear of Missing Out) and overbooks herself, this has helped me IMMENSELY. Initially, it was very hard for me to say no to things even though I didn't have the energy, but over time it's gotten easier. It's still super hard sometimes, but because I know from past experience how much better I'll feel, it makes it easier.

Just this weekend I attended a wedding and was planning to go to the after-party. Because I have social anxiety, being in social gatherings expends more energy for me. I usually NEVER miss a wedding after-party, but for the first time I decided to head home. I decided I'd create my own after-party. And, boy, did I end up having a restful Sunday the next day. In fact, on Monday (today as I'm writing this), I have been more productive than I have been in weeks! I got so much done at my workplace, I sat down to work on this book three times today (which NEVER happens in one day), and I even did a live video interview.

Typically, after a working day and a live video interview, I am zapped for the day. But I went for a walk afterward, cleaned two drawers in my bedroom, AND came back to write (it is midnight now). Seriously, who am I? I don't even recognize myself! And that is the magic and power of managing your energy.

The Marble Technique to Manage Your Energy

There are a few steps to managing your energy, so let's start the process now:

1. First you want to simply observe these next seven days and notice your energy levels throughout the day. Notice when you have higher energy, notice when it is starting to dip, and notice when you are zapped out for the day.

2. Next, apply the twenty-five marble technique and start to assign marbles to how much energy you feel you expended. Maybe you had a team meeting today with your boss that expended ten marbles because you have massive anxiety when meeting with your boss.

3. Third, start to practice the twenty-five marble method in your daily life. You can even use a jar to drop the marbles as you use them. And then gift yourself some recharge time at the end of the marbles, or after every five marbles you expend. Get creative and have fun with it.

This simple process alone can work wonders for your energy levels. Here are a few more practical ways to measure and manage your energy:

- Check your energy levels midway in the day to see how to position the rest of your day. Over time you'll see patterns and know what works best for you. (Practical tip: set an alarm at 3:00 p.m. every day that says "Energy Check")
- Do things that nurture and nourish you.
- Surround yourself with people, places, and things that uplift you, make you smile, and fill you up.

Rest on Purpose

Most of us have no idea how to rest and do not rest enough. Our bodies needs space and time to heal and repair for optimal functioning. This requires rest. Getting a good night's sleep is great, but it's not the only kind of rest that is important.

Rest in the daytime. Rest between meetings. Rest before and after travel. Rest after having company over. Rest in between working on a long project. There are many ways to rest; you have to find what works best for you. You might wonder, *How much do I need to rest?* You will find those answers for yourself through your own discovery process.

As I started to observe my own energy levels, I would notice where my energy would start to dip, or what kind of activities would really drain me. The days that I had calls all day with clients, I was utterly exhausted and needed to make extra time for rest. I would notice when I would need a break, or I would practice scheduling breaks on purpose. Sometimes that break might be standing outside in the sunlight in between calls for one minute, taking a moment to stretch, or using the restroom.

Here's something interesting: Many times rest DOES NOT FEEL GOOD, especially in the beginning. The reason is that you are so used to being ON that resting is probably going to feel like shit. Often when I have a day off, I feel wired, like I need to log on to work, like I need to be doing something, and I feel low-key, frantic, and antsy. But usually by halfway or two-thirds of the way into the day, I have eased into rest. You might think that's a waste and think, *I only rested one-third of the day when I had a whole day*. It's definitely not a waste. Why? Because that last part of the day you rested ten times more because you were actually relaxed.

Once the true rest comes, it feels wonderful, and you'll be so glad you did it—even if the beginning felt a little crazy.

Managing Your Time

My coach told me she did not like attending kids' birthday parties, but she felt she had to like it to be a good mom. It was stressful just being there and pretending she was enjoying herself. One day she got honest about this and brainstormed other ways her children could attend without her. She found a solution, and it was a game changer for her. It lifted so much tension, freed up her time, and allowed her to spend her time in a way that was valuable to her, even if other moms disagreed.

A number of us are spending our time in a way that isn't aligned to us, and that itself is causing stress in our bodies. We are doing what we think is expected of us, or things that are important to our relatives, peers, colleagues, and not always important to us. Spending time in a way that is meaningful to you will create more space and content in your life. This was a profound concept to me when I first learned it. I didn't realize how much more joy I'd experience from just adding pockets of time doing more of what felt good for me. Sometimes this meant music festivals, and sometimes this meant choosing to stay home rather than attend a hangout everyone else was going to (even though my FOMO made it hard sometimes!).

For some of you, the idea of spending your time in a way that you want may sound bonkers to you. Your schedule is full of appointments, family obligations, work commitments, and more. But here's the truth: You are probably spending time doing things you think you have to do that you could probably delegate or be more efficient with. But doing this requires knowing how you want to spend your time.

Most people have no clue how they want to spend their time. The majority of us are living on autopilot. We wake up and do the same things every day on repeat. We follow the same routine, experience the same stressors, and after a while it all starts to feel like a big blur. We feel disconnected from ourselves and soon fall into a slump.

Here's the great news, though: There's no real blueprint for life. We may have been sold one, but you can actually create your own. You might say you are limited because of xyz situation with work or home, but I want you to challenge your current routine, regardless of what limitation you might feel is there. Because the minute you decide it's not possible, you've blocked the 1 percent chance that it *is* possible.

Consciously spending your time in a way that matters to you, even if it's only 1 percent of the time, can be very empowering, and it helps you to feel more centered and grounded. Your life feels more meaningful when you live on purpose and with intention.

Think about what matters to you. How would you want to spend your time if you could do anything? The following questions will help you uncover some of the answers to these questions as well as provide some great journaling and reflection prompts.

Journal and Reflection Questions

1. How do you currently spend your days?
2. How do you spend your weekday?
3. How do you spend your weekend?

4. What are five things that matter to you?
5. What are five things you want to spend time doing in your life?
6. How do you want to spend your days?
7. How do you want to spend your weekday?
8. How do you want to spend your weekend?
9. How would I spend my day if no one was watching?

Exploring Your Current Time

At first, as you explore your life, you might realize that you do a lot of things out of a sense of what you think you should, what people will think, or because that's all that you know. This awareness or realization about your own life might feel traumatizing at first. Here's what I want to offer you. You have been doing the best you could with the knowledge you've had. Instead of judging yourself, approach this exploration with curiosity and compassion. I will remind you of this MANY times throughout this book because you might find yourself in judgment every other moment—and that's OKAY too.

This was one of the biggest breakthroughs I had when my cousin passed away. I realized I was doing a lot of things I didn't want to do because I thought I had to, and I was doing less of what I truly wanted. As I slowly started to add more of what gives meaning to me into my life, my stress levels decreased, and my joy levels increased substantially.

Value-Based Time

Managing your time based on your values and desires is a life-changing experience. You will gain your power back with time instead of feeling like you are always at the mercy of it. To do this, you will first observe how you currently spend your time, then consciously decide how you WANT to spend your time, and use your creative zone of genius to make it happen. As you start saying no to things that you don't feel aligned with, you will create more space for what you do want.

This will be on an ongoing project, so don't expect this to happen in one week. Over time you will notice things, make small tweaks, and then more tweaks as you grow and change over time. Don't worry about the destination; instead focus on this present time, this day, this week. I am continuously observing and tweaking how I manage my time. One thing I value a lot is space in my schedule. So I purposely create pockets of time where I have no plans and nowhere to go. It's honestly my favorite activity—doing nothing.

I saw a funny TikTok video clip where the voiceover said, "If I tell you I'm doing nothing, it doesn't mean I'm free. It means I'm doing nothing." That is so my jam.

The twenty-four-hour exercise below has changed my life in so many ways. I'm excited for you to complete it and find new discoveries for yourself. This is an activity you can revisit and do every so often, as your answers might change over time. It's a great road map to help you create the kind of day that is meaningful to you.

Activity: The Twenty-Four-Hour Exercise

1. Observe your last twenty-four-hours. How did you spend it? Hour by hour—write it down. It is important to actually write it out and not just think about it.

2. Map out how you'd spend the last twenty-four hours of your time here on Earth. Rehearse a scenario in your mind where if you knew the world was ending in twenty-four hours, what would you do? In this world, absolutely anything is possible, and you have all the money, resources, magical abilities you want and there are no limits. I invite you to get as bold, crazy, and ridiculous with it. Dream big. Dream silly. Let it all out and be

truly honest with yourself. What would you do if no one was watching? No one has to see this vision but you.

3. Arrange more of your days to include time for activities that you'd do on your Last Day on Earth map. Maybe in your last twenty-four hours you want to be on a boat, so how can you spend more time with or around water on a daily basis? Even if that means in your backyard, by the park, or even in your bathtub! Maybe you want to be with a loved one or dance at a party. How can you include more of that in your daily life on purpose?

I started doing this simple exercise after my cousin passed away, and it has done wonders for my mental health and happiness. I am no longer constantly dreading each day, waiting for a better future "one day." I am creating that better future in my current day now, even if I don't have ALL the things I want. I remind myself that our time on this Earth is limited, and I decide that I want to make each day count.

I often think to myself, *If I unexpectedly passed away tomorrow, would I be proud of how I lived today?* If the answer is no, I allow myself a redo the next day. The more I've done this, even with a 1 percent win, the better my life feels. This doesn't mean I don't have horrible days, or I don't get depressed and upset, but it does mean I am spending my time more consciously with intention rather than just on autopilot.

These small fundamental shifts can give you back so much time for what truly matters to you. And that's how you find yourself living a more meaningful life.

Removing Time Wasters

There are likely some things you are doing that are a complete waste of time. They are not useful and are only draining you. One example is worry. Worry is a huge time waster. It is not productive, it doesn't send you into creative solutions, it only keeps you in the loop, and it sometimes paralyzes you. This doesn't mean we shouldn't worry, as there are times that worry is useful, but we shouldn't spend all our time worrying. It drains our energy and doesn't add anything valuable to our life most of the time.

> *Worry is like a rocking chair; it gives you*
> *something to do but never gets you anywhere.*
> ERMA BOMBECK

As you dissect and investigate your time, notice what time wasters you are indulging in. This could also be social media scrolling. It could be writing and rewriting the same paragraph in your book fifty times rather than sending it to someone to review after the eleventh revision for feedback.

Now, here's something very important I want you to realize. The idea of time wasting doesn't mean you SHOULD be doing SOMETHING all of the time. It just means being intentional with your time. So, if there are periods of your time where you are doing nothing, it may not mean you are wasting time. It could be your intentional resting time, and that's fabulous. Having pockets of nothing time is actually VERY productive because you are recharging your energy. Then, when you come back from intentional free time and resting, you will have more energy.

Do not rush the process. This will take some time to look at for yourself. But start to notice and observe where you might be spending time in ways that are not useful, productive, or meaningful to you.

And here's the best part—you get to decide your time wasters. There is no ultimate answer of what is a time waster and what isn't. For some people social media scrolling is relaxing and a way to disconnect from work. So don't assume what you might think is obvious, instead dig deeper, ask why, and decide what is important to you.

Managing Your Space

Have you noticed that when you clear your space, you feel so much better? A cluttered space equals a cluttered mind. There are three aspects of space we will explore: physical space, mental space, and energetic space.

Your Physical Space

Notice how you keep your home space, your work space, and your car space. How can you create your space in a way that nurtures and delights you? Did you know that beauty and pleasure (you get from your space) is a form of self-care? When I learned this, I became more conscious of how I enjoy my space, and that includes when I am traveling.

Your Mental Space

What is constantly going on in your head? Are you constantly spinning your wheels? Do you ever give your brain a chance to breathe? It's important to explore your mental space, clean it up, and feed your brain possibility. Some great ways to do this are to go on a walk, journal, or listen to podcasts or inspiring music.

Take time to declutter your mind space, customize your personal space, and give yourself space. White space in our brains gives us a blank slate to come up with creative solutions and solve problems.

Your Energetic Space

You know when you're in line at a grocery store and you can just feel someone behind you? They are not touching you, but you can feel it. They are in your personal or energetic space. I've read that we can only physically see about 10 percent of ourselves, which means there's 90 percent of us that we can't see. We want to be mindful of who and what we let into this space and continually protect our energy.

Once I was doing a session with my healer, and she told me my energy was crowded and there were one hundred people in my bedroom. One hundred people's energy! I was like *How do I get them out?* This is when I realized how important energetic space is. Because we are energetic beings, we connect to one another deeply. Someone tells you a horrible thing about their day, and that energy can come home with you.

A few great ways to clear your energetic space is with palo santo, sage, crystals, incense, and high vibrational music.

The Awful and Awesomeness of Life

No matter how much self-care you practice, and how many positive affirmations you speak to yourself, some parts of life are just going to plain suck—and that's okay. We have to be able to embrace the suck rather than hope that life will be 100 percent amazing one day. Will it get better? Sure, but there will still be sucky parts.

A concept that I learned in my certification training at The Life Coach School helped me immensely around this. It's called 50/50: 50 percent of life is awful, and 50 percent is wonderful. You may find you've had days like that too—when you experience an extreme high and low at the same time.

I was watching a speaker on stage, and he told us it was a profound and magical moment for him. He was getting to speak on stage in front of 1,500 people. And at the same time, someone close to him passed away that morning.

Everyone has this human experience—even wealthy people. People often believe that being rich will solve all their problems, but rich people experience the same human problems and roller-coaster emotions as anyone else. No amount of money can stop the human experience from happening.

Whenever I remind my clients of this concept of 50/50, the relief I witness on their faces is amazing to see. That it's OKAY if half of our life sucks. The pressure we put on ourselves to be perfect and happy all the time can be awful, adding a whole unnecessary layer of suffering!

A wonderful tool as part of your self-care kickstart is to ask yourself, "How can I embrace both the awful and the awesomeness of life?" Sometimes that's through gratitude, sometimes through laughter about the irony of life, and sometimes through just allowing yourself to cry through the sucky parts. It's all a part of this beautiful thing called life.

PART TWO

Formula

CHAPTER 4

The CARE Formula for Stress Management

Stop measuring days by degree of productivity and start experiencing them by the degree of presence.
ALAN WATTS

A man in the audience asked me a question, and my friends gasped. They were holding their breath, hoping I'd be able to answer it. It was my first time delivering a stress management talk, and they knew how nervous I was. They had come to support me.

"This sounds like a great tool for in the moment stress, but what about longer-term stress that doesn't go away overnight, such as a mother who has a son with depression, or someone in an abusive relationship, or ongoing financial struggles?"

I took a deep breath and responded with what I knew to be true. My friends were relieved. They told me afterward how worried they were and how they hoped I would be able to answer the question on the spot. The man asked a great question: Essentially, does this tool work only for short-term stress or long-term stress too? The answer is yes.

What I responded to him was that when we are in stress mode, in fight-or-flight mode, many of us cannot think clearly or support ourselves from the best place whether for another person or even for ourselves. If you are in an ongoing stressful situation, you can use this tool to reset your system, and then lead your day and make decisions from a cleaner head space. So, no matter what situation you find yourself in—whether a one-time event or an ongoing one—this tool will come in handy. And in addition, this tool will help you practice greater self-care and create healthy long-term habits.

Seasons of Care

Caring for yourself is a momentous dance. Sometimes you will amp up, sometimes slow down. I like to think about caring for yourself in cycles like the four seasons.

There is summer, winter, spring, and fall. Winter contains the resting and hibernation months. Spring is for new beginnings and fresh starts. Summertime is about growth and activity. And Fall is about harvest and expression.

When I find myself overworking and overdoing, I remind myself that even nature has four seasons and needs its rest for the winter. It's a great reminder to help break out of the nonstop go mode. Many of us operate as if we are always in a summer of growth and activity, and that is not sustainable— hence the reason so many of us are sick, burned out, and overwhelmed! We are not meant to be constantly doing, and we have to remember this. It's easy to get into a robotic mode of nonstop doing without realizing it. Especially when everyone around you is doing it too.

You can associate each of the four seasons with a phase of self-care you can practice. If you're not sure how to self-care, this is a simple blueprint to guide you.

We can use these cycles to help remind us to:

- cleanse (spring)
- nourish (summer)

- recharge (winter)
- express (fall)

How to Care for Yourself

Caring for yourself means being your own best caretaker. That could look like tuning in to yourself, holding space for yourself, and taking appropriate care that feels right for you in the moment. It might feel odd initially, and that's okay. You might even feel a little cuckoo talking to yourself, and that's okay too. It's a relationship you will build with yourself over time. Soon you will become your own best friend, one you can count on. That is true care. It may not be perfect or easy, but this skill will take you far.

Being your own caretaker means listening to your needs and desires. There is a part of us that wants to belong, be seen, heard, acknowledged, and more. When we don't honor or feed these parts of us, we can feel helpless, out of control, and insignificant. Often these needs will come out through connecting with your inner child. Your logical mind will tell you what you "should" think or feel, but your inner child will tell you what's really going on in your heart.

> The concept of the inner child was first proposed by psychologist, Carl Jung, after he examined his own childlike inner-feelings and emotions. Jung postulated that it was this inside part of all of us that influenced all we do and the decisions that we make. Inner children were us when we were kids that never grew up. (CPTSD Foundation)

When I felt depressed, broken, and defeated, one thing I found extremely healing was holding compassionate space for my heavy emotions. I started listening to my inner child and what she had to say. I gave her space to come out and pout, scream, yell, and whine, in privacy with myself. I gave her space to breathe when she felt suffocated inside. When she told me how much life sucked, I asked her what she needed and how I could support her. I would listen to her answers and respond as best as I could.

Sometimes she wanted to stay in bed all day and cry, and I let her do that if I could. Sometimes she had no desire to go out, but there were some events that "adult me" wanted to attend. I had to negotiate with her how long we would stay or how I could make the experience pleasant for her. Sometimes that was through asking her what she wanted to wear. This made the inner hurting part of me feel seen and heard and it allowed "her" (me) to express herself, essentially, allowing my spirit to express itself. It's almost like I was in partnership with myself rather than dragging myself through life.

It was a painful yet beautiful healing journey to bond with the part of me that was hurting inside. Of course, I couldn't deliver all of her requests, but I made sure she felt heard and taken care of as best as I could. It was the beginning of a new friendship between us—me and myself. Creating this container of care within myself has been one of the most healing parts of my journey. It's almost like being your own safety blanket, knowing that it's there whenever you need it, without judgment.

Letting Your Body Do the Heavy Lifting

I learned from a Shaman (medicine woman) that sometimes our body processes things for us that we don't have the emotional capacity to handle. For example, if you are going through heartbreak or grief of losing a loved one, you may get really sick right around that time. The emotions are just too heavy for your mind to handle, so your body helps you in processing the pain through sickness.

This made me think of getting sick in a whole new light. Instead of getting mad at my body for getting sick (especially at inconvenient times), I learned to honor and thank it. Our body helps us to purge, cleanse, and heal.

Every time I had a cold, my healer would always tell me, "Your body is releasing sadness!" Sometimes I wouldn't even know what I might be sad about, but she would tell me to just honor and care for my body as it released something that had been stored in me potentially for years.

The body has a natural healing ability and knows how to come back to homeostasis, our normal state. Think about when you have a bruise or cut, and how in over a week your wound heals itself. Or when you have the flu, and your body regulates itself and slowly comes back to health.

Getting sick is also another way for our body to grab our attention. Many times, we work past our limits and don't rest enough. Sometimes our body has to send us a signal to slow down. Have you noticed that sometimes you get sick right when you have a big project going on or large commitments?

Our bodies are powerful healers and process emotions in various ways—sometimes through tears or hair loss and sometimes through illness. I had to remind myself of this multiple times when I got mad at myself for being sick. The next time you find yourself in this space, let your body do the heavy lifting for you and nurture it back to health. This has been a beautiful self-care practice that has helped shift my relationship with my body—to express gratitude for it rather than being angry at it. Honor your body and thank it for doing the work for you.

CARE FORMULA: The Stress Management Tool for Daily and Long-Term Stress

The year I started delivering stress management talks, I burned out multiple times. It made me feel like a fraud. How could I be teaching these tools and burning out myself? It reminded me how easy it is to get swept up in the overworking culture because it is often the norm.

When the world around you is constantly moving, you feel like you need to keep moving. When others around you aren't stopping, you feel like you shouldn't either. You start to think you are a super-human and can do all things. That is, until your body comes crashing down telling you otherwise.

The tool I am about to teach you is the stress management tool I use in my daily life. I am teaching it to you in a four-step process so your brain can digest it and comprehend it. But the truth is, when you use it, it may not always go in a perfect linear order—and that's okay. Life is not linear, and it's the same when using this process.

The CARE Formula

The CARE Formula is created for you as an acronym, so it is easy for you to remember. Each letter represents its own care step. This is how it breaks down:

C - Compassion: Practice **C**ompassion toward yourself.
A - Attention: Pay **A**ttention to what's going on.
R - Recharge: Stop to **R**echarge, reset, and reflect.
E - Engage: **E**ngage with the situation in a way that feels aligned to you.

I'm going to share with you how I used this exact tool to write THIS book. Bringing this book to life has been stressful. It was a very vulnerable and uncomfortable process. I probably wrote twenty-six drafts before I got to this final one. I felt extreme agony in the process and wanted to quit many times. I was surprised at how hard it was for me. This tool helped me get to the finish line, and here we are today. You can use this example and apply it to any situation you have in your life, even intense ones.

Real Life Example: Moving through Stress to Write This Book

Weeks after I signed the contract with my book publisher, I rented an Airbnb in Siesta Key, Florida, a ninety-minute drive from where I was living at the time. With my love of road trips and exploring new areas, I thought it was the perfect way to enjoy the writing process, which felt extremely daunting and isolating at times.

I remember J.K. Rowlings had rented a hotel room to write her final book in the Harry Potter Series, *Harry Potter and the Deathly Hallows*. I had heard of writers going on writing retreats to write their book, so I was excited to create my own writing retreat!

The Perfect Plan

As I was getting closer to the weekend, I realized I had no real plan. I decided to create an intention and schedule. My goal was to write for twelve hours over the course of the weekend, six hours on Saturday and six hours on Sunday. And I would spend the evenings exploring Siesta Key and Sarasota. It was the *perfect* plan. I was going to spend the weekend there and write, write, write in a peaceful area with beautiful views.

I had picked an Airbnb that was slightly more expensive because I thought, *If I am going to write in this place, I have to feel inspired.* One of my joy triggers is beauty, especially in the environments I am surrounded by.

As Friday afternoon rolled around, I was tired from work and wanted to take a nap, but I still had to pack and drive ninety minutes to my Airbnb. I didn't have much energy. I didn't feel inspired. In fact, I felt burdened by this trip. That evening I had to be gentle with myself because I could hear my inner child starting to complain. She was tired. We were tired.

The next morning, I woke up with zero desire to write. The idea of writing for twelve hours on the weekend sounded dreadful. It sounded nice in theory, but now it felt like punishment. I beat myself up in my head. *What are you doing? What do you mean you don't want to write? Are you stupid? You spent all this money on this luxurious Airbnb with a beautiful view to be inspired to write!*

It was torture. I was literally fighting myself in my head. If you've been inside your own head when you're fighting with yourself, you know how painful this can feel. One part of me was cursing at myself for being a person who didn't follow through on her plans, and the other part of me was crying dry tears inside like a sad seven-year-old because I didn't want to do it.

Step 1: I practiced compassion.

I realized that nothing was going to move until I took a pause first. So that's what I did. I stopped what I was doing and acknowledged that I felt stressed.

I reached for compassion for myself. I honored that I was struggling. Doing just this calmed my nervous system down a few notches. It was almost like I felt heard by my own self. I was my protector, and I heard her call. Then I decided to go for a walk outside.

Step 2: I paid deeper attention.

On my walk, I paid attention to the fight going on inside of me. I noticed how it was unproductive. No side of the argument was winning, and we were just in a standstill tug-of-war. I continued to ask deeper questions, and then it all clicked. I realized that I was exhausted from work this week and hadn't rested yet!

I had seen a ton of clients, been on back-to-back zoom video calls, and my cup was empty. I was trying to jump from a full work week to a full work weekend. I felt depleted. No wonder I had no desire to write! I was literally forcing myself to work on this book while my inner gas tank was empty. What I needed was a day off! Connecting with myself allowed me to understand the stress that was going on inside me.

Step 3: I decided to recharge and reset.

My body already started to relax once I had this new realization that I needed a day off. I could breathe again. It made sense that I needed a break before I could dive into work again. Funnily enough, I was bummed about spending all this money on the Airbnb and not being able to enjoy it since I was going to be working. But now I had the chance.

All of a sudden, my mood shifted. I went from being a sobbing grump to an excited little kid. Within minutes I was blissfully swimming around in the private pool, taking selfies, and playing my favorite reggaetón jams on my Bluetooth speaker. I am known for taking my Beats Pill+ speaker everywhere! Hearing music with a good bass just gives me life. I had no idea how much I needed that playtime after a long stressful week.

It felt so therapeutic to be floating in the water. I looked around and soaked in the entire view. I was in awe of the beauty. I told my best friend about my insight, and she affirmed it was a good idea to take a break. "What kind of self-care book are you writing if you're burnt out yourself?" she jokingly said to me.

"You know what? That's a REALLY good point!" I told her. We both laughed. It put things into perspective for me, and I realized I was doing the right thing: taking care of myself.

Step 4: I was ready to engage.

After spending some time in the pool and clearing my head, I was ready to get out. There was no longer a tug of war inside me. I felt ready to write.

I now had the mental and physical capacity to work on my book. I decided to let go of the rigor of my plan. The plan made me feel trapped and then inadequate for not being able to follow it. This was a huge relief to my system.

I took a shower, changed my clothes, and sat out on the back porch and wrote my heart out. The view was just so incredible, with the pool and the Gulf waters behind it.

I felt nurtured, grounded, and whole. After I wrote for a few hours, I got dressed up and went out for the night. I explored the Siesta Key Beach area, downtown Sarasota, took myself out to a lovely dinner at an Italian chophouse, and then went to a couple of bars!

I went from a grumpy grouch to a productive writer to Dora the explorer. Writing this book has been teaching me how to self-care. And that's how I used this stress management process in real time to write this book!

Now let's break down the steps further so you know how to use it for yourself.

The 4-Step CARE Formula

Step 1: Compassion

Stop what you're doing and connect to yourself. In this phase, you need to recognize and acknowledge that you are feeling stress. And then choose compassion toward yourself. This has been a life saver for me in many intense situations. It might take you a moment to get to compassion, but focus on feeling it.

One way to practice compassion: You can put your hand on your heart and say to yourself, "I know you are stressed, and I love you anyway. It is safe to feel this. I see you. We are going to be okay. I love you."

This might seem silly when you first start doing it, but you will see what wonders it can do. Just acknowledging the stress you feel starts to reduce it down a few notches. When we avoid our stress, it only makes it more intense.

Main question to practice compassion: How can I be kind to myself right now?

Step 2: Attention

Drop into your body and allow yourself to feel what is coming up for you. Notice your thoughts, your feelings, your body, and your breath.

Your emotions are a vibrating sensation that are moving through your body. It's like your body is a tunnel that the emotion must pass through to get to the other side and release. Thinking of it like this makes emotions feel less scary, especially ones like anger or sadness.

One way to pay attention: Focus on the sensations floating through your body. Take a moment to describe what it feels like. Then identify and label the emotion you feel. When you do this, it reduces a layer of stress because your body is no longer freaking out in the unknown. You have now told your body what is going on, so it starts to calm down.

Say to yourself, "It's safe for me to feel this emotion. It is part of the human experience and simply wants to pass through me. I am not my emotion; I am simply feeling an emotion."

Questions to dig deeper: What am I feeling right now? What is bothering me? Where do I feel stress (or this emotion) in my body?

What does it feel like? Describe it. What does my body want right now? How can I feel supported and nurtured?

Main question to pay attention: What am I feeling and thinking right now?

Step 3: Recharge

In this phase, you take a break from the situation at hand and filling up your cup. This will look different for everyone and will be customized to you.

One way to recharge: Disconnect completely. This could mean physically or emotionally. Take a moment to step away from the situation or from digital devices. Go outside for five minutes. There is nothing like nature to rejuvenate us. Allow yourself to reset and reflect.

Questions to dig deeper: How can I disconnect right now? How can I energize myself right now? What do I really need right now?

Ways to recharge: Go on a walk, stretch, call a friend, take a bath, turn your phone on airplane mode, spend time with a loved one, sit on a bench and people watch. You will find many more activities listed in Chapter 7: Recharge.

Main question to recharge: How can I fill my cup right now?

Step 4: Engage

In this phase you are redirecting your energy into a new place. You've transformed the stress by acknowledging it, naming it, and this in turn created some space in your mind and body.

Before you decide how you want to engage in your life, with yourself, or in a certain situation, allow yourself to think about all the possibilities available to you. Don't limit yourself. Even if you think it's not possible, ask: how could this be possible?

This space is where the magic happens. Where creativity is born, and solutions are made. When you are ready, decide what step you want to take next. Sometimes the next step could simply be to do nothing and be present with your current self right now. That is a decision too.

One way to engage: Ask questions, think about the possibilities, make a decision, then engage. Ask yourself: What do I know to be true? What matters to me the most? What do I really want? If anything were possible, what are some solutions I could execute? What are five different possibilities I could run with? What are the pros and cons for each? Which one do I feel most aligned to? What's one step I can take right now? How can I make that even easier?

Main question to engage: What's one step I can take right now?

The CARE Formula helps relax your nervous system, clear your mind, and give you some space to decide what feels right for you. It's okay if you don't find a solution right away, but you will now have created the space for it to come to your mind. This is a plug-and-play version of the CARE Formula you can use on the spot.

You can also use this formula to practice self-care on the daily. For example, every day you can practice compassion toward yourself, pay attention to your energy levels, feelings, recharge your body, and engage in life or with your day. Over the next four chapters, we are going to dive deeper into each step and provide you more concepts and tools to take your self-care practice further.

CHAPTER 5

Compassion: CARE Step #1

If your compassion does not include yourself, it is incomplete.
BUDDHA

When I was living in California, I drove down to Orange County for a conference. I booked a nearby Airbnb so I could get there early and get a good seat. The next morning, I was running late. I was so frustrated that I started cursing at myself. In that moment of rage, I could not feel anything else. I could not think straight.

As I was getting closer to the venue, I realized how tense my body was and decided I didn't want to take this energy into the conference with me. I wanted to enjoy the event. It was Chalene Johnson's Marketing Impact Academy event that only happened once a year.

I skimmed my mind for some coaching tools to help me through this moment. Anything I tried wasn't working or clicking for me. I felt helpless and got more frustrated. After some time passed, I decided to surrender and just be with this anger I was feeling. Since nothing was working, I decided to reach for compassion toward myself.

I spoke to the part of me that was hurting inside, "Baby girl, I know this is so hard for you right now. I know you are struggling. I know you are trying your best. And you're doing it, baby girl. You are here. You made it happen. You are attending this conference. I know you are upset about being late. But you know what? I love you anyway." And that did it.

I immediately burst into tears as I felt compassion spreading like a warm blanket throughout my body. I felt seen and heard. I felt so much lighter after I let go and held compassion for myself. I walked into the event less angry, more surrendered, and more open. You won't believe what happened next.

When I entered the event hall, someone I had met the day before had an extra seat in the front row and waved to me to come sit next to her. After I sat down in utter disbelief and joy about my front-row seat, someone from the VIP section walked up to me and offered me her VIP goody bag, saying she didn't want it. Excuse me? What was happening? In that VIP bag, I got gifts worth over two hundred dollars. Once I chose compassion, my day completely turned around. It truly blew my mind.

Compassion heals. Compassion awakens. Compassion touches the heart. Compassion reduces stress. It's fascinating to note that Buddha, after years of trying to reach enlightenment, finally attained it after he felt compassion while watching ants as he was lying under a tree. **Compassion is that powerful.**

Compassion Opens Doors

That conference experience taught me a valuable lesson: When all else fails, reach for compassion. I could not shift anything on that drive there. Nothing was working. None of my coaching tools, mindset hacks, nothing. I was filled with stubborn rage, and nothing was moving it. In that moment, the only thing that worked was compassion. I had to let myself be with the emotion, to accept it, to surrender to it. Once I brought the compassion in, it opened up the doors for me. It was like a floodgate of emotion breaking through a dam in a river. The dam represented the stubborn emotion. And the water represented the emotion underneath like sadness, exhaustion, or whatever else was there.

I had a client named Sunny who told me she started a coaching program to feel better. She wanted to feel more connected to her kids and have more joy. She was midway into her program and said she felt none of that. She felt only rage. And she felt it often. She felt rage toward herself, her life, her kids, her husband. She told me she knew she "should" be more grateful and appreciative, but she wasn't and didn't know how to be.

I shared with her how our emotions are there for a reason and aren't there just to torture us. They are our messengers. I asked her, "Instead of pushing the anger away and judging it, how can you lean into it?" Her eyes opened up. "Wow, now that you say that, I realize I really do judge myself. I am very harsh with myself."

I asked her how she could invite compassion into this. How could she be compassionate toward herself and her rage? What was her rage trying to tell her? Was she working over her limits? Was she not setting boundaries? There was something there for her to explore deeper.

Before she dove in any further, I could tell that the compassion had already done wonders for her. Her shoulders were less tense, her face looked more relaxed, and there was a sense of calmness in her aura. She had compassion for herself and was no longer in a fight with her true feelings of rage. It's amazing how compassion alone can shift something in us.

The first step to caring for yourself is always compassion. Compassion awakens. Compassion touches our heart. This is not just a theory but is actually backed by science. If you remember nothing else from this book, or forget what self-care is, just remember to choose compassion.

Why Forcing Gratitude Doesn't Work

You might hear this advice when you are hurting: "You should be grateful. Look at all that you have to be grateful for. You are more fortunate than others." While these comments are well intentioned and sometimes helpful, they usually aren't.

When I was struggling emotionally, a handful of peers told me I should be more grateful for what I had. They were right. But as much as I tried, I was not able to feel grateful. I felt misery. Instead, this created a superficial layer of forced gratitude on top of my suffering. And surprise, surprise, the suffering didn't go anywhere. In fact, trying to push it away caused the suffering to grow bigger.

On top of that, now I felt shame for my suffering. I felt like something was wrong with me for not being able to feel grateful. *Why do I feel like this? Why can't I just be happy with my life? What's wrong with me?*

The shame I felt around my suffering made me feel less than, made my struggles feel insignificant, and made me feel deeper pain. I felt like no one understood me or my pain. I couldn't talk to anyone about it because it felt like no one was on my side. I didn't feel supported. So instead, I suffered in silence and just shut down inside. What I have learned is that when you are hurting, your pain (and your inner child) wants to be seen, acknowledged, and heard.

There is no room for gratitude when you are in pain. Instead of trying to force gratitude on yourself, give your suffering some compassion. This can shift your energy and alleviate tension. Allow yourself to hear yourself out. Let your suffering air out. Allow it to breathe. Whether that's through talking, journaling, or art.

If you don't feel safe with anyone to let the suffering out, you can create that safe space with yourself and also work with a professional coach or therapist. I did both. I worked with a professional and also learned how to hold space for my pain. I learned how to validate my feelings even if no one else agreed or understood. It's important to be able to hold space for your own emotions because no one else will do that for you. This is part of becoming your own best friend that you can rely on.

I believe there is a place for gratitude in the self-care journey, but there usually isn't space for it when you are charged up with heavy emotions—especially ones like anger, sadness, or defeat. You have to make room for gratitude, by first starting with compassion. Then when you are ready to process your pain, even just 0.2 percent of it, it will create room to experience gratitude. As I've processed my pain over many years, it has truly allowed me to feel a lot more grateful for the things I do value in my life.

Journal and Reflection Questions

1. How often do I feel grateful from 1-10 (with 10 being very grateful)?
2. How grateful do I want to feel? Why?
3. Do I force gratitude on myself? Why or why not?
4. What are some ways I'm forcing gratitude on myself? Why or why not?
5. What does grateful mean to me?
6. What does grateful feel like?
7. What am I grateful about? Why?
8. What am I not grateful about? Why not?
9. What do I want to be grateful about?
10. From 1-10 how much suffering do I feel (with 10 being great suffering)?
11. What do I feel suffering about? Why?
12. What heavy emotions are sitting in my heart?

13. What emotions am I ready to process?
14. What do I want to feel?

How to Have Compassion

- Speak kindly to yourself.
- Observe with curiosity instead of jumping into judgment.
- Validate your feelings. Have empathy for your struggles and pain.
- Create a safe space for you to feel all your emotions.

Scientists have found that being kind to yourself actually lowers stress hormones, boosts the immune system, and increases your lifespan.

Saying kind words to myself has been a saving grace for me in some of my toughest moments. When I have said, "I understand why this is so hard for you, and I love you anyway," it made me feel seen and heard during difficult times when I felt alone in my pain. It calmed down my nervous system immensely when I was in a high stress state.

Notice next time you are beating yourself up about something you did, or something that happened, or a mistake you feel you made, catch yourself and stop midway. And instead offer compassion to yourself. This doesn't mean that you won't look for ways to improve in the future, but this does mean that you will stop being mean to yourself in the process.

Some people think that beating themselves up constantly will force them to strive to be better. Maybe this works for some people, but for most it doesn't truly work. When you feel like shit, you don't want to do anything to improve, or you operate from uninspired energy. Bringing yourself compassion first relaxes your nervous system and allows you to have the space to engage from a more grounded, centered place rather than from fear or a foggy brain.

Journal and Reflection Questions
1. How kind am I to myself from 1-10 (with 10 being very kind to myself)?
2. What are ten ways I can be kind to myself?
3. What are some kind phrases I can say to myself?
4. How often do I judge myself from 1-10 (with 10 being very often)?
5. How can I lead with more curiosity instead of judgment?
6. Do I have empathy for my struggles and pain? Why or why not?
7. How can I have more empathy for my struggles and pain?
8. Do I feel safe to feel all my emotions? Why or why not?
9. How can I create a safe container to feel all my emotions?

Giving and Receiving Compassion

"I know I just met you last week, but I just want to tell you that you matter to me," she told me. Those words meant everything to me in that moment, and theystill do. It touched me beyond belief when I was really struggling.

In my Master Coach Training Program, I shared with my peer coach that I was struggling with feeling like I belonged and that I mattered at all. These were very painful, deep wounds that were rising to the surface from my past. She held space for me as I laid all my vulnerable stuff out on the table. Just saying these words out loud felt so freeing. Being witnessed like that is so powerful, often for both parties. I felt so much healing that day.

This is why I find coaching to be SO powerful. It creates space for you to face all of you, even the parts you hide from the rest of the world. When you are witnessed, seen, heard, acknowledged, it can free you from a stronghold that has been keeping you stuck or small for decades. It offers a new perspective and a new opportunity.

The compassion I received from her was truly healing for me. I wanted to share this story to illustrate the power of giving compassion, and also the power of receiving compassion. Whenever your heart is open to offering someone compassion, go for it; it will be healing for both of you. And whenever someone offers you compassion, open yourself to receive it.

Journal and Reflection Questions

1. What are ways I like to give compassion?
2. What are ways I like to receive compassion?
3. What are some ways I can give compassion to others?
4. What are some ways I'd like to receive compassion from others?

What Is Self-Love Really?

The idea of self-love feels like a stretch for many people. What does self-love even mean? The idea of loving myself sounds nice, but it feels weird. The best way I have simplified self-love for myself is to think of it in this way: **Self-love is acceptance.**

When you can fully accept yourself, that is love to me. "You are this way, and I love you anyway." When I find myself in a difficult moment, accepting myself goes a long way. And if I am not able to accept myself, I will just say, "I accept that I don't accept myself right now, and I love you anyway." Do you know how freeing that is? Trying to force yourself into acceptance becomes an internal fight. So just accept that you are at a place of nonacceptance right now.

Find Ways to Love Yourself

One way I like to love on myself is singing loving songs to myself. I will listen to a love song and actually sing it to myself. Or I will imagine this is the universe or the Divine singing it to me. Just today as I was driving back from the dentist, I was jamming to a song called "Unconditionally," by Ajebutter22. He talks about unconditional love. I am a huge lover of Afrobeats music.

Singing love songs to myself fills me up with love, and lets me catch a vibe and a better mood. Look up the song and try it out yourself.

What are some creative ways you can love on yourself and show yourself love?

You get to decide what self-love means to you and what it looks like for you. Allow yourself to do some discovery on this. Remember there is no right or wrong answer. Use these questions to simply explore and create your own version of self-love that you can tap in to whenever you want to.

You can answer one or all of the questions. You can use these as journal prompts on different days. Allow yourself to be creative and use your imagination. There are no limits to these questions.

Journal and Reflection Questions

1. What does self-love mean to me?
2. What does self-love look like?
3. What does self-love feel like?
4. If self-love had an image, what would it be?
5. How do I practice self-love?
6. How do I want to practice self-love?
7. What is love?
8. How do I feel love?
9. What makes me feel loved?
10. How do I express love?
11. How would I like to express love?
12. How do I receive love?
13. How would I like to receive love?
14. How can I create more love in my life?
15. How can I feel more love in my life?

Practicing Acceptance

Acceptance creates an opening.

There are a lot of things in the world that we cannot change or control. Ultimately the only person you truly have control over is you. Practicing acceptance can go a long way in reducing stress.

There are moments when I have wanted to change things about myself, but many times it was a way of rejecting myself the way I was. I have had to learn how to practice acceptance so I could meet myself where I was. I had to learn how to practice acceptance as I learned my own traits. I got to learn how to practice acceptance even around the things I didn't like about myself. I realized it was OK that I didn't love ALL of me. It was okay that I hated certain parts of myself and also liked certain parts. All of it is okay.

Making peace with how I felt about myself helped reduce a lot of stress and stop fighting what was happening inside me. It's like I wanted to love myself and like myself more, but I didn't, so then I rejected myself for not loving myself enough, which really just went into a whole new negative spiral. Rejection upon rejection.

The more we can practice acceptance, the more peace we can have inside. I know it sounds easier than it is in practice. The main thing to focus on is the fact that it is indeed PRACTICE, so anytime you're struggling with acceptance, remind yourself that it is a continuous practice that you will come back to—sometimes even twenty-three times in one day.

Don't think you have to be a Zen master of peace that accepts all. That is not what this is about at all. You are a human. You are going to have intense emotions, unpleasant emotions, and feelings of anger and rejection. This is simply a practice you can come back to when you are done fighting inside or realize you have no control over other people.

Accepting things and accepting ourselves doesn't mean we don't want to change or grow. Think of it more as a surrendering to what currently is in this moment. It is looking at the current situation and not running away or avoiding it. It is accepting where we are so we can ultimately see what else is possible.

As I'm writing this, I am chuckling because I am the queen of running away and avoiding pain and discomfort—like most of us humans! So, here's to telling you it's okay if running away and avoiding is what is working for you right now. But at some point, it may no longer work. I've come to this juncture many times. When I realized this, I was done running away from a certain situation, whether it was myself or something outside of me. Once I had made that decision, I gained the courage to face it, and that is where I was able to first come to an acceptance of what is, before doing anything else.

The reason acceptance is powerful is because it shifts the energy inside of you from avoiding and resisting to flowing. Acceptance drops that second layer of suffering we add on by rejecting the current situation. We are stressed, and then we are stressed about being stressed. What if we were to accept that, yes, we are stressed right now, and accept the current situation rather than trying to change it right away? Accepting it lets one layer of stress to fall away so we can go deeper to the real stuff underneath.

Acceptance also allows you to explore deeper, understand yourself better, and create decisions from a fresh perspective rather than from a place of avoidance and resistance. Acceptance is a door that opens up many more doors. You don't have to know how to do it, but just have a willingness to consider the idea of acceptance, and work your way up from there with reminders, repetition, and building new beliefs.

Journal and Reflection Questions
1. What do I accept about myself?
2. What do I not accept about myself?
3. What would I like to accept about myself?
4. What am I having a hard time accepting about myself?

5. What do I accept about others?
6. What do I not accept about others?
7. How would I like to be more accepting of others?

Giving It Over to Love

"Giving it over to love" is a concept I learned from author Tosha Silver, and has helped me a ton when I feel stressed or am in a difficult situation. Tosha is the author of *Outrageous Openness: Letting the Divine Take the Lead*, which is one of the most profound books I have ever read.[1] At times when I feel too overwhelmed by something and feel powerless, I will give my problem/issue over to love. Love can be whatever you want it to be. An energy. Mother Earth. The Universe. God. Electrons. Spirit Animal. Your Soul. The ocean . . .

Giving over my conflict to something bigger than me allows me to let it go. Even if only 0.5 percent lets go, anything helps! It allows me to loosen the grip I have on a situation. Today I coached a client who was feeling tense about a situation that happened at work. Her fists were clenched with emotions of anger, shame, guilt, and resentment all in one.

In a way, by talking it out she was giving it over to love. She showed an act of love for herself by facing the situation and asking for coaching on it, and that ended up releasing it out into the world by her saying it out loud. She said she felt immediate relief by just articulating it. She told me how grateful she was to have me as a witness to her, because it made her feel safe to let it out even though she felt crazy inside.

She was trying to hide her intense feelings by trying to keep the peace at work so she wouldn't be blamed, even though the situation was not her fault. Once she gave it over to love, and talked it out, she felt relief, and from a calmer space she was able to make an informed decision how to handle it at work.

Outrageous Openness has become my manual for life. I keep coming back to it to help me in tough situations and allow love to lead me. Practicing Tosha Silver's concepts has helped reduce my stress immensely. When I share some of her tools with my clients, they often find them very useful. Her work has changed my life, and her book has helped me gain greater compassion for myself and the world around me. I highly recommend that you add it to your next reading list if this idea resonates with you!

The main question to ask: How can I offer compassion and kindness to myself right now?

So, what if the highest expression of the personal Divine is You,
precisely as you are in this very moment, in all your
full, authentic, wounded glory?
TOSHA SILVER, *OUTRAGEOUS OPENNESS*

CHAPTER 6

Attention: CARE Step #2

*The greatest gift you can give yourself is a little bit
of your own attention.*
ANTHONY J. DEANGELO

Agatha is a manager at a retail store. She found out tht her employees were talking negatively about her. She was hurt and angry and came to me to get coached on what happened. She was in a mental fog and unable to think straight. As she paid deeper attention to what was going on, we uncovered some deep wounds that were showing up from her past. We processed her emotions together, which created space in her brain to reflect on what to do next.

While reflecting, she realized there were a lot of things throwing off the dynamics with her team. One was that she was being their friend more than their manager. She realized there were some boundaries she had to set in place, and she needed to be firm when speaking about her decisions. She also started roundtable discussions with her team to foster community and to get their input about what was working and what wasn't at the store. This made her team feel included, and it improved the overall morale at work.

By paying deeper attention, Agatha was able to reduce her stress, find mental clarity, and make a decision on how to move forward.

Had she made a decision from a place of feeling hurt, it may have not benefited her or the team. Allowing herself to step back and do this processing was a game changer for herself and her team.

Pay Attention to Your WHOLE Self

I would often find myself working on the computer for hours without taking breaks. But when I started paying attention to my body's signals and energy levels, I started to pick up on when my energy was slowly dwindling. I could tell that I only had a certain amount of energy left. Knowing that would guide my next decision and the rest of my evening.

Now I have a much better idea of how to take care of myself by having this information. I usually get a flash of it about two hours in advance, letting me know that's how much energy I have left. This lets me know that hey, I have one hour of energy left in me, so let me start packing up so I can leave by then, or if I feel ready to leave, I go early. You might notice you feel this when you are at an outing, event, or at someone's house. You feel an internal clock when it's time to go home.

Your body and emotions are messengers that will give you cues on what it needs. Whether that's through tears letting you know it wants to release, through cravings for certain nutrients, or through muscle aches telling you to rest. These are just a few examples, but your body's signals will be unique to you.

Notice when your body is wide awake. Notice when it feels tired. What lights it up? What drains it? What makes it want to dance? Get to know your body and start to build a relationship with it.

Spend time focusing on all areas of yourself starting with these four: mind, body, spirit, and environment. You might notice that you have a habit of paying more attention to one part more than the other. That's probably the case for a lot of us. See how you can focus more on other parts as well. Remember, even just 1 percent more attention to an area of your life will be helpful.

How to Pay Attention to Yourself

The best way to pay attention to yourself is to notice, observe, and listen. Pay attention to your body, your emotions, your thoughts, your actions, and your environment. Another way to pay attention is to give yourself space. For example, if you are feeling a heavy emotion, you can give attention to it, and give it space to breathe.

The simplest way you can pay attention to yourself is through presence. Pay deeper attention to parts of your yourself and your day. Notice how your body tenses up before a certain meeting, or how relaxed you feel when your friends are over. These are clues to help you care for yourself. It's showing you places to take deeper care of yourself, and also certain things your body and spirit wants more of.

You'll start to notice where you find yourself more stressed, when you find yourself more relaxed, and over time you will take note of these patterns. For example, you might notice that you have a low-key panic attack every time you travel. Once you notice this is happening every time, you can start to instill new habits to help you manage travel stress.

There are many times when I was in distress, in a difficult moment, or feeling trapped. One of the best ways through those moments was asking questions. This led me to find out how I could support myself by digging deeper. For example, let's say you're having a difficult evening, and you ask yourself, "How can I support you right now?" You might answer, "A bath and a movie, please." Answering that call for support can often do wonders for your spirit and nervous system.

Asking questions will help you uncover your self-care needs. You'll notice that once again I switch between first person and third person in some of the questions. This is on purpose because asking the questions slightly differently can uncover new answers. Remember, the quality of your life is dependent on the quality of the questions you ask.

Journal and Reflection Questions
1. What am I feeling right now?
2. How can I support myself right now?
3. How does my body feel right now?
4. What are you feeling right now?
5. How can I support you right now?
6. How does your body feel right now?

Get to Know Yourself

Connecting to yourself is a big part of self-care. Your personal self-care plan will be unique to you, and therefore, you have to know who you are (even if it's just a little bit). A big component of stress management is the skill of tuning into yourself.

Many people don't know who they are. If you were to ask them what gives them joy, what lights them up, they don't have an answer. There are many reasons for this. One is that most of us are living in survival mode just trying to make it through the day. Another is that we are encouraged to be helpers and be good people. But as we may tend to another's garden, we must also tend to our own. Being a good person is also about being a good person to yourself. In order to be good to ourselves we have to know who we are, and what we need.

We are so busy, caught up in our day-to-day lives, going after our next accomplishment, that we mainly identify ourselves by our line of work, our family, and where we grew up. The YOU of who you are is vastly bigger than that. We haven't had space to explore deeper. But now we have an opportunity to.

Journal and Reflection Questions
1. What is your view of yourself?
2. How do you think about yourself?
3. Where do you put yourself first?
4. Where do you put yourself last?
5. When do you work past your limits?
6. Where do you work past your limits?

Ask "why?" to each of your answers to continue to dig deeper.

Pay Attention to Your Thoughts

Your thoughts have a direct influence on your stress levels. A situation can happen, and you might make meaning of it, creating a thought loop in your head that causes you stress. It will play continuously in your head for the next ten years. That is, until you decide to stop this thought loop by paying attention to your thoughts, and consciously release the one that is no longer serving you. Perhaps it's a judgment toward yourself, someone, or something.

As you start to pay attention to your thoughts, it might be overwhelming to see what you find. You may realize how mean you are to yourself, or how your thoughts make you feel super sad. You might even feel shame or anger once you start paying attention. This is all a normal part of the process. Nothing has gone wrong.

This is why, as you do this work, it's super important to practice compassion. Hold a safe space for yourself to see and explore your thoughts. Allow yourself a judgment-free space inside yourself as you explore.

I've experienced this myself. Sometimes I would get very upset once I became aware of the dialogue looping inside my head. Some inner dialogue you will find up front, and others will be more hidden. Those will require deeper digging to find. Why do we want to find them? Because some of those background thoughts can be what is leading to greater stress or anxiety on a daily basis.

For example, if you have a thought loop like "I'm never going to be enough" playing in the back of your head, it is draining your energy and probably creating anxiety in certain situations. Discovering these thoughts can help you consciously identify what you want to keep as part of your mental mindset, and what you want to shift.

The great thing is that once you do release a thought loop, it creates space in your brain. You will feel free because this thought loop is no longer keeping a grip on you and holding a tension inside of you. Isn't that beautiful?

But before you let go of any unconscious thoughts, do some deeper digging, because that exploration will give you a better understanding of where this loop came from, how it has served you, and it will help you have deeper compassion for yourself.

My Master Coach always stops us as soon as we want to throw our unwanted thought in the garbage and try to grab a new one. She would say, "Don't be in such a rush to change your thought, because that won't last long without fully processing through your current thought loop and emotion. It exists for a reason!" And she would invite us to explore it fully before practicing stepping into a new conscious thought loop.

As I explored my own thought loops, I found a lot of negative chatter happening in the background. It helped me see how I was wearing myself out. I was literally exhausting myself by having thought loops playing in the background that were draining my energy and causing me massive anxiety. Some thoughts that people in my coaching practice have discovered include "I'll never be enough; I don't matter; I don't belong; I will never do that again. I hate myself; It's too hard, so why try anyways? I hate my life; I'm not smart enough; I'm never going to get through this; that event scarred me for life; nothing ever works for me; I will never get to have that. . . ." The list goes on and is unique to everyone.

What do you do once you uncover these deeper layers? Ask questions. And more questions. And more questions. This rabbit hole will help you see where you are, allow you to process through some it, then consciously decide what you want your thought loops to be. What kind of words and information do you want to be circling in your head all day? For example, I want to create more thought loops in my head about myself that empower me, help me get through each day, and fuel me with energy and inspiration.

Journal and Reflection Questions
1. What kind of thoughts ruminate in your mind a lot?
2. What kind of thoughts do you have the minute you wake up in the morning?
3. What kind of thoughts do you have at the start of your day?
4. What kind of thoughts do you have throughout the day?
5. What kind of thoughts do you have at the end of the day?
6. What kind of thoughts feel exhausting?
7. What kind of thoughts give you energy?
8. Where do I find myself in scarcity thinking?
9. How can I think in abundance and possibility?

Pay Attention to Your Body and Feelings

We have been told, "There is no time for feelings" and that we should put away our feelings in the workplace, or even at home. But feelings directly influence how we show up, how we make decisions, and the results we create. Think about how you show up when you feel good or calm versus how you show up when you're tired and angry. Whichever fuel you are running on will affect the results you produce. Your feelings are what fuel you. In fact, your feelings are the most important thing you should be paying attention to.

Many people are afraid of feelings. But truly the worst thing that's going to happen is just a feeling. When I am drowning in a painful feeling, I often try to remind myself that this is just an emotion passing through me; I am not going to die. This feeling will pass. It can be helpful to remind yourself of that when you feel trapped in your emotion and don't see a way out.

Paying attention to your feelings will allow you to navigate your stress levels better. It will give you signals to your current state and what you may need right now.

Journal and Reflection Questions
1. How does your body feel?
2. How does your body feel in the morning?
3. How does your body feel after eating a meal?
4. How does your body feel in the middle of the day?
5. How does your body feel after work?
6. How does your body feel in different environments?
7. How does your body feel around different people?
8. How does your body communicate with you?
9. How does your body give you messages?
10. How do you feel your body's intuition?

Process Emotions

This is one of the most important self-care skills you will use for the rest of your life. I really struggled with this because I was never told it was okay to have emotions. I was scolded for my emotions, taught to hide them, or encouraged to get over them.

We are taught to keep it together, to be pleasant and nice. We are not allowed to be angry or too emotional. This causes us to suppress emotions, but they don't end up going anywhere; instead they end up getting stored in our bodies.

Not facing my emotions is exactly what led to my facial paralysis when I was twenty years old. When I looked up the emotional root cause of this condition in Louise Hay's book *You Can Heal Your Body*,[2] I discovered that Bell's Palsy is caused by suppressing extreme anger. When I thought back to that time in my life, it was true—I was suppressing anger about a situation in my life.

Being able to process emotions is one of the most important skills you will learn and use forever. Life takes many twists and turns, and we will have emotions about it. This is part of human life. We want to start embracing our emotions, rather than pushing them away.

Our emotions have messages for us. They are directing us. They are showing us our truth. It may be inconvenient, and it may be unpleasant initially, but essentially our emotions are what will set us free.

So how do you process your emotions? There are different ways to process emotions, and I'm going to give you one of the main ways that you can do it.

Processing an Emotion

1. Start by taking a few deep breaths and dropping into your body. You can imagine a green ball going from your head into your heart or your stomach. Remind yourself that it's safe to feel this.
2. Notice the sensation you feel in your body and where. Describe it.
3. Identify and name the emotion. This itself decreases the intensity because your body is no longer freaking out and wondering what's happening.

4. Allow yourself to fully feel the sensation of that emotion in your body for sixty seconds with no distractions. If it helps, you can put your hand on your heart or stomach as you do this to help with any intensity.

5. Take a deep breath and release. Imagine this emotion moving through your body and out. Even if just 1 percent leaves, that is a release, and you've created some space inside yourself.

You'll be surprised at how helpful a simple technique like this can be in a difficult moment.

Other Great Tools for Processing Emotion

- *Emotional Freedom Technique (EFT) or tapping.* I use tapping a lot to help me process emotions. Check out the resources link at the end of this book for more information on this, including a tutorial.

- *Free writing:* Just writing out whatever your heart wants, allowing yourself to be as raw and vulnerable as possible. Then you can throw the paper out when you are done or burn it in a fire.

- *Creative project:* Engaging in some sort of art or creative activity can help process emotions. Whether that's drawing, painting, or writing poems. You'll see a few of my poems in this book that I wrote to help me in certain moments.

Allow yourself to get creative in ways to process emotions, but you can always come back to the five-step process I shared above.

What to Do When It Feels Too Painful to Face

When I started my Master Coach training, we had to complete self-coaching homework. The very first week, as I was exploring some of my own inner limitations, I hit a block. I couldn't go deeper. The belief that I found lived inside me, made me feel numb inside, and quite frankly devastated me. I couldn't believe what I uncovered. I asked my coaching peers that week how to go deeper because it just felt TOO painful to face. At the same time, I wanted to because I could see how it was holding me back from my potential.

I ended up getting coached on this topic a few days later. I will say that processing it with someone else made a major difference for me. It was too hard to explore that on my own. It felt too scary, a path I could not walk alone. Having someone on the other end felt like a safety net, and seeing her warm compassion and curiosity it feel less scary to explore.

When it gets too painful to face, there are a couple of options you can choose. One could be setting it aside and coming back to it later. Another could be talking it out with a trusted friend. Or it could be working with a therapist or coach to face it.

Do you need to face it? You have a 100 percent choice in what feels right for you. For me, I wanted to face it because I knew this had been holding me back for a while, and I was ready to take my life to the next level. But I knew these old stories, habits, and traumas were hard to break, and I needed support. So I voluntarily wanted to face it because I was ready. Also, I noticed that doing this work on my own was taking a lot longer, and that working with a coach and in a program would help accelerate finding my own inner blocks and having the support to move through them.

How to Connect Deeper

Connecting with yourself and building a relationship with yourself is one of the building blocks of self-care. You may have heard that cliché phrase "The answers are inside you" and rolled your eyes, because what does that even mean? I don't have any answers inside me; I need HELP with my problem. TELL ME THE ANSWER! But the truth is that no one but you has the answers for you. There is a personal uncovering process that you have to go through. People may have suggestions, ideas, or examples to share, but ultimately the answer has to be aligned to you.

There is a gold mine within you. It has the answers to your struggles, problems, and worries. You may not believe that right now, and that's okay. We have been taught to seek answers from the outside. It is part of how we've been conditioned to live. This is part of where the disconnection for us happened.

After my cousin passed away on my birthday, it triggered an existential crisis within me. During this time, I started asking myself deeper questions. Once I uncovered answers about things I wanted to be doing, then I asked myself, "Well, why aren't you doing them?" The answers that were revealed to me were very informative.

I discovered that I was holding myself back for a mix of reasons: my own personal insecurities, fear around the unknown, and other people's opinions. I didn't realize the depth of how this was stopping me from living the life I wanted to live.

To help me with this jarring realization, I bought the book *Untamed* by Glennon Doyle.[3] In the book she talks about trusting the voice inside of you and stopping the stressful efforts of trying to constantly meet everyone else's expectations.

Blocks to Connecting with Ourselves

One block to our connection with ourselves is that we are impatient. We want answers now. But unfortunately, this digging process will take its own time. Sometimes the answer may come sooner, other times later. Trust the process. It is like an unveiling that happens the more you go within.

Another block to our connection is our unwillingness to admit the truth. The truth sets us free, but it can also isolate and ostracize us. It can be scary, painful, and difficult. Sometimes it takes until you are in your deepest pain that you find the courage to face the truth.

Use the following activities to explore yourself and get to know yourself better. Later you will use some of your answers to build your own self-care plan. If you find yourself getting lost in the exercise and spending too much time on it so that you overwhelm yourself, stop and do this instead.

Dedicate a simple twenty-five minutes to each exercise and make yourself stop so you don't exhaust yourself. Some of these will be ongoing questions to ponder in your mind. As you move through the day, you can always come back and add more to the list. If you can't decide and find yourself overthinking, just make yourself pick something. Decision fatigue is a real thing. More on that in an upcoming chapter.

Questions to Connect Deeper

Here is a list of questions that will assist you on your inner exploration and connection.

- Why do I do that?
- What am I making it mean?

- What is my true feeling?
- How am I feeling right now?
- What do I really want?
- Who is the person I want to be?
- What feels right in my heart?
- Would I regret not doing this?
- What are the pros and cons of each?
- Which am I more drawn to?
- If I knew the answer, what would it be?
- What would I be doing if no one was watching?
- Who would I be if no one was watching?

Activities to Connect Deeper

The Big Five Exercise

Think about what five big things you want to experience, have, or accomplish before you die. These five things will be completely different for everyone. Some might be related to being at a certain weight, traveling to certain countries, hitting a milestone in your career.

One of my big five is writing a book. So, by the time you are reading this I will have accomplished one of my five big life goals, and I can die happy. That feels pretty amazing.

Think of your own examples first by thinking deeply about your desires. Notice any programming that comes up in your mind. Notice if you think, "Oh that's stupid, that's frivolous, or I should have something more noble." No, you shouldn't! None of it is stupid. This is your life, and you get to choose how you want to live it. That is such an empowering thing to realize.

Allow yourself to go there. Dream big. Dream bold. Or dream simple. Whoever YOU are, connect to that. But know that in this exercise there are no limits. So have fun with it.

Getting to Know Yourself Exercise

Answer these questions and feel free to come up with more of your own. Allow yourself to write down whatever comes up first. Then later if you want to add more, you can. But don't overthink it. Just write.

- What's my favorite color?
- What kind of clothes do I like to wear?
- What kind of outfits are my favorite?
- What are my favorite cuisines?
- What are my favorite dishes?
- What do I like to do in my free time?
- What kind of people do I like to surround myself with?
- Who inspires me?
- What inspires me?

My Favorite Things List

Inspired by the last one, name your favorite things. Make a list in your phone or in a journal. It will be fun to go through life identifying what your favorite things are. Favorite color, favorite kind of movie, favorite dessert, favorite self-care activity, etc. And if the idea of this is stressing you out, know that you can change your favorite things any day you want. It is not permanent! Have fun with it!

Here's a sample list to add in your favorites; feel free to add more favorite things based on your unique self!

Add your favorite:

- Color
- Quote

- Dessert
- Book
- Movie
- Restaurant
- Travel destination
- Outdoor activity
- Cuisine
- Food
- (keep adding to this list with your own categories!)

The main question to ask: How can I pay deeper attention to what's going on for me right now?

The pins
The needles
That poked me
From your words
Creating wounds
That are waiting
Waiting to be filled
With Divine love
To remind me
I'm not damaged
Just simply
Bruised
And ready to heal
Heal me Divine one
ADITI RAMCHANDANI

CHAPTER 7

Recharge: CARE Step #3

When we drop from the busyness of the world it allows us
to come home to our hearts.
TARA BRACH

The last weekend of writing this book before turning it into my publisher was brutal. I think it was my initiation to becoming an author. I had never written that much in a few days in my entire life! One thing I noticed was the self-care I found myself practicing. I literally took many baths and showers in those few days to reset and rejuvenate.

I would notice when my energy was dwindling, and I would need to get up. One time I was at Panera Bread working on this book for five hours. I tried to keep going because I had a deadline to meet, but my brain was mush. I decided to get a twenty-minute chair massage as a way to reset. Then I jumped in the pool for twenty minutes. Next I took a bath. When I got back to writing after that, I was a whole new person.

Resetting myself in between writing sessions was huge in helping me finish this book. In the past I would have never done this. I was known for working on the computer for six-plus hours without a break. *Horrible, I know.*

This step is all about recharging, resetting, and reflecting. This is where you rejuvenate your mind, body, and spirit. This will be something you build in your ongoing self-care plan and remember to do when you find yourself stressed.

Reset and Reflect

Reflection is a powerful care tool because the perspective it can give you can move mountains for you. It can solve problems in your head, heal pain, and give you new ideas to approach something. Reflection reminds you of what truly matters to you and gives you deeper clarity.

When and How to Recharge and Reset

We need to be charged just like our electronic devices. This is why sleep is an important part of our daily routine. Our bodies and brains need space and time to rest and repair. Notice how much time you are spending each day being "on." Are you spending equally that much time being "off?"

I believe we need to recharge way more than we currently do. This can look different for people, and there is a list of recharging activities at the end of this chapter. At a very minimum recharging looks like getting an adequate amount of sleep. For some that might be six hours, for others twelve hours. Notice for yourself what amount of sleep feels optimal for your body.

Create time to reset and recharge every day. Or make space for it once a week or a month. Resetting can look like taking stretch breaks in between work meetings or getting some sun every morning and evening. I recommend sprinkling recharge activities throughout your day, even for as little as one minute. It can also look like taking a day off or a week off to simply rest. You will test and trial activities to see what feels good for you.

Stepping Back

Sometimes we need to take a step back and allow ourselves to reset before we can re-engage with a situation. Once we've given the issue/problem/stressor the attention it needs in the last step, now it's time to let go and relax or play. Tuning away from the stressor allows you to reconnect with yourself.

You may have resistance to taking a break in this step because we are conditioned to keep going in the hustle culture many of us live in. You may want to bury yourself in work or another task because this problem has really rattled your insides. Instead of the temptation to throw yourself into something else, allow yourself to be with the discomfort of it. It will be well worth it, because when you are fighting what is causing you discomfort, it's more tortuous. Let yourself feel the discomfort and walk through it anyway. This will cause less pain in the long run, even though it might feel like the opposite.

Activities to Recharge and Fill Your Cup

There are so many recharge activities you can choose, either from the list below or a list of your own. I've helped many of my clients create practices designed specifically to their desired goals. Other clients choose an activity that they feel aligned and called to.

You can choose to do one of these techniques for five minutes every day, or you can choose to try a different one every few days. Make this practice yours and have fun with it. There is no right or wrong here; there is simply practicing self-care. You are winning regardless of what you choose!

Emotional Freedom Technique (EFT) or Tapping

This is an acupuncture-based practice where you tap your fingers on meridian points on your body including on your face (temples, under eyes, chin) and body (chest, underarms). This helps reduce your tension, anxiety, and stress. It is one of my favorite tools. You'll find a tutorial video in the resources section of this book.

Walking

Walking helps release stuck energy that is sitting in your body, gets your blood flowing, and can be very therapeutic. More than the physical benefits, I find that I get a lot of mental benefits from walking. Walking gives my brain the space to process thoughts, consider ideas, and cleanse itself. I also find myself with some mental peace and clarity after a walking session. It also helps to blow off steam when needed!

Journaling

You can use this to empty your thoughts, to-do lists, and frustrations onto paper. There is something powerful about transferring information from your brain to paper that creates some space in your brain. Many of my clients find journaling to be therapeutic. I also have a handful of clients who do not like journaling at all. Try it and see what works for you!

Dancing

This is such a good way to shake up and shake off your day. It can add some joy and smiles as well as be a perfect release for tears and tension. You don't have to know how to dance at all! You can simply jump up and down and move your body to the right and the left.

People Watching

This is a great way to lean back and relax. Let your mind wander and stare into space. Giving your brain some white space to breathe is healing!

Poetry

Writing poetry has helped me through some of my hardest moments. Poetry gave me that outlet to express, process, and release my pain. I've used poetry to help me through breakups, the passing of loved ones, even daily frustrations. You don't have to know a special formula to write a poem to use this as a recharge activity. Just write what flows out of you.

Yoga

An ancient practice that has so many benefits that cover all areas of mental, physical, spiritual, and environmental. It helps relieve stress, center your mind, and connect deeper to yourself.

Coloring

When I started seeing adult coloring books in the stores, I was overjoyed. I love that we as adults get to be included in this fun activity. It's become one of my favorite ways to de-stress, unwind, and process through some mind knots. Grab a coloring book from your local store, get some colored crayons, pens, markers, whatever floats your boat—and get coloring!

Gardening

My dad loves to plant flowers at our home every summer. If this brings you joy and relaxation, go and garden! If you don't have a garden or space for one, allow yourself to be creative. Maybe just get a plant or two.

Cooking

My mom is a huge fan of cooking. She makes the best food—Indian food, Italian food, and Asian food, all of it. She enjoys it. Cooking can be a huge source of joy and stress relief for many people. If this is something you enjoy, do more of it. And if you're short on time or ingredients, make it fun and easy in your own creative way.

Napping

It's crazy what a twenty-minute power nap can do for you. Whether you are a napper or not, it's something to try. I remember one day after the beach, I was beyond exhausted, but my relatives were all hanging out in the backyard. I decided to plop on the couch and watch TV to unwind. I ended up falling asleep for about thirty minutes. After I woke up, I joined them at the pool, and I had a whole new energy. I was amazed because an hour ago I had felt completely numb and dead. Ever since that day, I've believed in the power of naps.

Appling Essential Oils

I love essential oils. I love using peppermint oil and lavender oil. Just these two oils have helped me so much. They relax your nervous system, regulate your moods, and awaken your senses. I especially like to use them at the beginning of work to invigorate my senses, energize, and awaken me, and to unwind at night after work.

Relaxing Baths

I never used to take baths. Now this is my favorite thing to do. I cannot tell you the amount of relaxation, cleansing, and creativity I feel from a bath. Sometimes after a long day of clients, I feel really crazy. I just lay in the tub for a little while, and it feels like all the heaviness just melts off me. Water is very purifying. Sometimes when I am stuck on a problem, I take a bath, and oftentimes when I come out, I have a new idea that has popped into my head.

Deep Breathing

Slow, deep breaths can do wonders to reset your mind and body. My favorite breath is a simple 3-3-3. Pull air in through your nose for three counts, hold it in for three counts, then push out from your mouth with a small circle for three counts (like you're blowing focused air to a certain area, so you keep your mouth in a small circle). I do this with many of my clients, and in the self-care circles I lead to help people ground in and also unwind at the end. Sometimes people attend my self-care circle in a scurry, running to the computer after just arriving home. After we do this breathing, everyone is centered, and everyone's face looks calmer after they do it.

Earthing

Earthing is a technique in which you come in contact with the Earth's natural charge and experience being grounded. This releases inflammation naturally and prevents chronic inflammation.

Essentially, the earth has a healing vibration it gives off, which is backed by science. Check out the book *Earthing: The Most Important Health Discovery Ever!* to read more.[4] Ever since I learned about Earthing, I've been spending so much more time outside barefoot— especially when I'm in between calls or taking a break from an activity. I always feel recharged and refreshed afterward. Try it!

Self-Inquiry—Asking Questions

Self-inquiry is definitely one of my major go-to tools in my self-care journey. It is what leads me to me: parts of myself I haven't met, parts of myself I am building, and parts of myself that are being released. It also creates room for new ideas and directs you to what matters to you. Very powerful work!

You can answer the various questions that are posted throughout this book to start your self-inquiry journey. Come up with your own questions as well as you practice curiosity and observe yourself with compassion. Lastly, you can also Google "self-discovery journal prompts" to find more ideas.

I send monthly self-care reminders to my readers, which often include topics of self-inquiry and reflection. If you'd like to receive these, you can sign up for free at this link: www.AditiCreative.com/selfcarenotes. (Also found in the resources link at the back of this book)

Some Great Questions

- What am I making it mean?
- What if this weren't true?
- What's one thing I can work on that would enhance my entire life?
- What really matters to me right now?
- How would I like to spend my time?
- What recharges me?
- What makes me feel full inside?
- What's another perspective?
- What is the worst thing that can happen?
- What is the best thing that can happen?

Inner Child Meditation

I lead people through an inner child meditation in some of the self-care circles I lead with groups. Many times, people have told me afterward that they have never been able to connect with their inner child or go that deep before.

I recorded an audio version of this meditation for you as well, which you can find in the resources section at the end of this book. I've also written a mini version of it here:

> Imagine you are walking through a forest, and you come across a stump. At this stump you see a child. It is you. Pick an age that feels right. Ask this child version of yourself what they are struggling with, what's on their mind, and how can you support them. Listen, and just let your heart speak. Then allow yourself to speak back to your child self and share anything that you think would be helpful. Hug your child self and tell them that you're here anytime they need you. Walk out of the forest.

Parking Lot or "Worry Time"

My Master Coach shared with us how she decided one day she was going to stop saying unkind words to herself about a certain experience. She realized how much suffering it was causing her, and she just decided she wasn't going to beat herself up in this way anymore.

This idea was amazing to me, I felt intrigued by it. I wanted to stop doing this too, but at the time, I was finding it difficult. So, instead I got the idea to do a parking lot. I decided I was going to put a PAUSE on worrying about this topic, and I "put it in the parking lot" for a few months. This simply means putting this topic of conversation on hold for now and coming back to it later. Essentially it is a "virtual" parking lot in your head.

This felt doable! I went ahead and tested it out. Every time my brain would think about it, I'd be like, "NOPE. Remember we said we weren't going to think about this until September?" Then I directed my brain to think about something else that was also on my mind. So far this has been working beautifully, and I'm not beating myself up or worrying as much I was in that certain area!

What do you do when September rolls around? You can investigate and reflect how this time of pausing went for you and decide consciously what relationship you want to have with this topic going forward. And ten actively work on creating that new version or hybrid version of it for yourself.

Take Yourself on a Date

This is probably my favorite charging and getting to know yourself activity. I also consider this an act of self-love. Although all of these suggestions are, this one is a sure way to love on yourself and treat yourself.

Before you tell me that you don't have funds to take yourself out, or you feel it's a frivolous expenditure, here's what you need to know: You don't need to spend even one dollar on your date.

You can decide what to spend or not to spend, but ultimately it's not required. During some of my heavy depression times, there were many moments I only had twenty dollars in my checking account. So, believe me when I say that it doesn't have to cost anything.

There are many times I have taken myself to the park, to the ocean, or to a lake. I've taken a blanket, a book, water, and a snack. Some of the best moments of my life have been on the dates I've taken myself on.

On the other hand, I have also taken myself on more lavish dates like the spa, a top-notch restaurant, or a Broadway show. Have fun with it and make it yours.

Organizing

This can be a form of stress relief for a lot of people. It gives them joy and pleasure to organize. I enjoy the end result more than the process —although I try to find joy in the process too!

Laughing

Watch a comedy show or funny YouTube clip that makes you smile.

More activities to recharge:

- Cleanse/declutter/throw out old stuff/keep what matters
- Shift your focus
- Meditation
- Therapy
- Art
- Read an article or ten pages of a book
- Visualization
- Celebrate yourself

This book has many recharge activities to care for yourself. Start with what feels most right for you NOW and come back to the other stuff. If you are just looking for something to start, start with the top five ways to up your self-care discussed in Chapter 3: drink more water, move your body, go outside, disconnect and declutter, and pursue what makes you feel alive.

The main question to ask: What's one thing I can do to recharge and reset myself right now?

CHAPTER 8

Engage: CARE Step #4

*Saying yes to happiness means learning to say no to people
and things that stress you out.*
THELMA DAVIS

A few of my TikTok videos went viral, and I got so overwhelmed with all the comments that eventually I just put the phone away and hid. It was too much. I decided I did not have to respond to everyone—or anyone at all. It gave me so much relief because I thought I had to until I realized I didn't. My favorite thing about engaging is that you get to make the rules. You get to decide how you want to engage with the world, with yourself, and how you want to engage in self-care.

Engaging is where your self-care comes to life. This is where the magic happens. Where the solutions are born. Where your intentions come to life. This could look like making a decision on handling a one-time stress event, creating and executing your long-term self-care plan, or creating boundaries in your relationships.

After recharging and reflecting, you create space to engage. Whether that means listening to your inner voice, moving forward with a decision, or simply choosing to stay still and present with your current state. Maybe it means moving forward with a decision to change jobs because that feels best for your mental and physical health, or it could mean choosing to stay in your current situation and finding new avenues within your current role.

Engaging will look different for each person and for each different scenario. But mainly you want to engage in a way that feels right and true for you. This is where we make decisions, take actions, and create things. Create self-care routines, projects, take self-care actions, communicate boundaries, implement a self-care practice, and more. Actions can look like choosing compassion, journaling after work, taking a break between zoom calls, etc. Make a decision to stay no to someone, or start waking up fifteen minutes earlier for me-time, as a small glimpse of what engaging could look like.

The Three Parts of Engaging

Engaging is an act of self-care, because you are putting into practice something that adds back to yourself.

The three parts of engaging are:

1. Making a decision
2. Making space
3. Acting on your decision.

Making a Decision

Every creation starts with a decision. Before we build something in our life, we must decide what that will be. We might not know the "how" just yet, but we can choose the "what." For example, when I lived in Washington, DC, my local yoga studio was doing a ninety-day yoga challenge one winter, and I decided I was going to do it. My decision is what led the rest.

Making Space

Once you've made a decision, it's time to make space for it to happen. This could mean physically, mentally, or energetically. Sometimes we aren't mentally ready for a change we've decided we want, so we have to prep our brains for it—like working through negative thoughts. Other times we might physically need space for it. Or clear trauma that is holding up energetic space within and around us.

In my ninety-day yoga example, I had to create space in my schedule to make it happen. Sometimes this meant waking up early to catch the 6:00 a.m. class, while other times that meant moving around my evening schedule so I could make it to the evening class. It was an ongoing task to make space to go each day.

Acting on Your Decision

This is the most important step because you could make a decision and make space, but still not show up and execute your decision, which defeats the whole point! For example, I decided I would do the ninety-day yoga challenge, and I even made space in my schedule to go. But now I had to actually wake up, change, pack my bag, and head to the studio. This requires its own skill and mindset because it can be so easy to not do something, especially when it isn't a habit yet. But over time, the resistance will be less, and it will get easier.

Ideal Scenario

Many times, when we find ourselves stressed, we end up in a negative mind loop where we are hyper-focused on everything that could go wrong. This is a normal reaction, and I want you to practice interrupting this mind loop. I also want you to ask yourself, "What could go right? What is the best-case scenario that could happen?"

For example, let's say you started dating someone new, but you're feeling stressed because it's bringing up trauma from your past dating experiences. Every other second you are stressing out about it ending, about them leaving you, and it all ending in a disaster. You've already assessed all the worst-case scenarios, and now is your opportunity to also think about the best case scenarios.

Best case scenarios could look like: *Maybe this time it's going to be different. Maybe this could be the best love I've ever experienced. Maybe this is the experience I've been hoping for all along.* I know you might be thinking, *I don't want to set myself up for disappointment by thinking something good might happen, but then it doesn't.* But why would you want to sit in disappointment, feel miserable, and stress yourself out about a possibility that MIGHT NOT EVEN HAPPEN?

Give your brain equal energy to both ideas. Marinate in the great possibilities as much as you marinate in the horrific possibilities. This breaks that stress loop, because it interrupts the brain's pattern of thinking in only one direction. It creates possibility and dramatically lowers your stress to know that you aren't doomed to only one scenario, but there are, in fact, options here!

Now, if it is a very deep trauma that you are circling in a negative mind loop with, you may want to work through it with a professional to help you through it—like a therapist, healer, or coach. Sometimes these loops are too hard or scary to work through on your own, and that's okay. Having someone be there to support or witness you can help dramatically. I highly recommend Sweta Iyer, a Master Healer and Chakra Specialist. She has helped me and hundreds of clients work through and heal a lot of trauma. I include her information and other practitioners I recommend in the resources link in the back of this book.

The next time, before you are about to engage in something, allow yourself to look at not only the cons but also the pros. Look at not only the worst-case scenarios, but also the best-case scenarios. Often, it's a fifty/fifty chance that either could happen, yet we put all our energy on the 50 percent that makes us freak out and lose our mind. Give your brain some relief by proposing new ideas. This also allows you to make an informed decision before engaging.

Feeling on Purpose

Did you know that your feelings can be influenced by you? That you can in fact feel ON PURPOSE? I never knew this and always thought I was at the mercy of my feelings. Many of my clients are afraid of their feelings. They are afraid their feelings will overpower them and take control of them. This is because they haven't created a safe space to feel. One way you can do this is by simply telling yourself, "It is safe to feel this. I am here with you."

Once you have given attention to your current feelings and processed them, there will be a space that gets created. From that space, you can create a new feeling on purpose. Our brains are wired to continue thinking the same thoughts and producing the same feelings repeatedly because it's our brain's job to keep us safe. It considers new feelings as dangerous territory.

Why do we want to feel on purpose? Because we have the opportunity to create feelings that serve us. If we could choose a higher quality gas for our car at the same price, why wouldn't we? It will allow our car to run more smoothly and get us to our destination with less detours.

Often while writing this book, my feelings have been of fear, overwhelm, and doubt. Can you imagine how much harder that has made it to write this book? I've had to create new feelings on purpose to help fuel me to write from a place of determination, focus, and desire. It has allowed me to create a container of love to write from so I can write from the best place to all of you. Sometimes that meant doing this work every day.

How to Practice Feeling on Purpose

1. Ask yourself, "How do I WANT to feel?"
2. Create space for this feeling.
3. Imagine how this feeling would feel. Feel the sensation inside you. Remember a time you felt this last.
4. Memorize this feeling—how it feels and where you feel it in your body.
5. Allow yourself to ignite this feeling through memory, thought, and visualization.

Thinking on Purpose

As you determine the feeling you want to feel, identify what thoughts fuel that feeling. For example, when I think, "This is beautiful," I feel calm inside. But when I think, "I hate that!" I feel anger inside. Our thoughts create our feelings. We can think thoughts on purpose that create a certain feeling we want to have.

In my Master Coach training, we really investigate our thoughts deeply and notice which ones are holding us back in our career, at home, or emotionally. I realized I had a lot of negative thoughts floating in my head that were unconsciously there. So now I've been working on being mindful about which thoughts I want to keep circling in my head, and which ones I don't. It's definitely not an overnight process, but the more you think thoughts that you want to think, you'll overpower the old ones and release them.

Intentional Living

Living on autopilot makes you feel more out of control. Living intentionally could mean having an intention for your day, or for your week. This means deciding ahead of time how you want to feel, what you want to focus on, and what really matters to you. How can you live your days with intention?

Because I have extreme social anxiety, focusing on an intention has helped me a lot. For example, if I was having massive anxiety about going to an event, I will decide what I will focus on. Sometimes I will say to myself, "This night is about me. It's about experiencing myself, experiencing this night, and allowing myself to find joy in small things." When I do this, I find myself more present in the experience. I might notice the beautiful architecture on the wall, or the wonderful painting, or someone's amazing outfit. Or I'll focus on my feelings as I'm walking through an event. How can I focus on feeling the expansiveness of this moment instead of all the negative chatter my mind might want to bring forth?

This is just one example; as I always say, take the concept and make it yours. Be creative with how you might want to create more intention in your days, different situations, and within yourself.

Your Self-Image

How you think about yourself directly impacts your life, your energy levels, and your self-care practice. Your self-image is your perception of yourself. How you view yourself, how you think about yourself, impacts how you treat yourself, how you perceive the world, and how you live.

Reflect on your self-image of yourself. Notice how it's serving you, and also how it's not serving you. Think and consider what your self-image is now, and what you may want it to be. It doesn't have to change. You might find that your current self-image is serving you well, and this emphasizes your need to connect with more of that. That's something you can explore for yourself.

The best way to get the most out of this work is to be truly honest with yourself. Don't answer these reflections with what you think or based on how you present yourself to the world. Answer them with the deeper stuff that maybe you would never have shared out loud with someone. That's where the transformative work happens—when you're willing to GO there.

Journal and Reflection Questions

1. What do I think about myself?
2. How do I view myself?
3. What do I like about myself?
4. What do I love about myself?
5. What do I hate about myself?
6. Where did I hear these things? (Connect your responses to where you've heard it—a specific person, a commercial, a peer)
   * Finding these answers will blow your mind and give you a whole new perspective about where your views come from.
7. What do I want to think about myself?
8. How do I want to see myself?
9. What do I want to like about myself?
10. What do I wish I loved about myself?

Answer why to each of the questions to go even deeper.

Premium Fuel

This concept that I learned in my Master Coach training was very profound for me in helping me with my self-image. In a workshop, my Master Coach taught us how to deal with people's comments directed toward us. We learned how to have a strong self-image so negative comments don't bother us as much.

When you are filled up with premium fuel, there is no room for another person's opinion to land within you because you're already full. You are filled up with positive self-image thoughts about yourself, so when someone brings something that is the opposite or hurtful, there's literally no room for it in your system.

This doesn't mean that you run away from constructive feedback. It means not having room for people's comments that aren't serving you. If someone has genuine feedback, that's one thing. But if someone is saying something hurtful, it won't bother you as strongly because you value your own opinion more than theirs.

This concept is especially helpful for people who get easily dragged down by others' comments toward them, whether they comment on your appearance, on your personality, or anything else. Fill yourself up with premium fuel and there won't be space for any unwelcome energy, and you'll be able to respond in a manner that feels right for you because you are full of inner strength.

Decision Fatigue and Making Decisions

Managing your decision-making process can reduce the exhaustion that comes from it. When you teeter-totter around a decision it can drain your energy. Think about all the decisions you make every day. Which ones can be eliminated, reduced, or moved to a different day of the week?

A common one that becomes stressful for some people is what to wear or what to eat each day. Since this is a recurring decision you must make every single day, how can you make this decision process easier? Maybe you decide Fridays are pasta days. That releases one meal decision out of your head, creating some mental space. At one point my coach decided she was only going to buy and wear clothes from White House Black Market. It eliminated so many decisions in her mind. I remember meeting another woman who wore certain colors during certain seasons, which I thought was creative!

Pay attention to what decisions you're making on a daily, weekly, and monthly basis. Notice how they affect your energy and take note when you spend a lot of time making a decision. See where you can cut down some of this time and energy by simply making a decision. See how you can simplify some of your decision-making processes.

Love Your Decision

One reason people sit in indecision is that they are afraid of making the wrong choice. This idea of right and wrong can cause a lot of agony. Allow yourself to play with creativity. What if there were no wrong decisions? What if all the decisions you make will ultimately lead you to exactly where you need to be regardless of the road taken?

Something I learned and found helpful is to decide that all decisions are equal, rather than one being better than the other. And then whatever you decide, decide that you will love it, in advance. Choose to love your decision on purpose. Choose the decision with your whole heart. If you struggle with the idea of failure, decide that there is no failure, only winning and learning. Or decide to embrace failure as a win, a closer step to where you are headed.

Decision Regret

Once you've looked at the pros and cons, analyzed them a million times, and talked to 304,902 people about what they think—there's really nothing more you can do except to just choose. Allow yourself to make a mistake. And if you regret past decisions, remember that the decision you chose at the time WAS the right one at that time for you with the knowledge you had.

Decision Due Date

Do you find yourself spending a lot of time in indecision? I do. I notice I waste a LOT of time in indecision. I keep going back and forth and second-guess myself a lot. A great hack is to make a due date for your decision. When I find myself in indecision for too long, I tell myself, "Okay, you can stay in indecision for now, but by Monday you are making a choice." Lately, I've been practicing just choosing SOMETHING and rewarding myself for making a decision. Sometimes just deciding is the win in itself! The added bonus is that it frees up brain space!

Decision Ownership

There are some situations we stay in because we are mentally or emotionally paralyzed. Maybe it's a relationship, a job, or a community club. Maybe something happened in our past that we cannot let go of. Just because you uncover something and think that something else is a better choice for you doesn't mean you are ready to go there or do that. There are so many times I had an idea of what I thought the "right" decision was, but I couldn't get myself to do it. I learned to honor wherever I was instead of shaming myself about where I wasn't. Whatever you choose is OKAY. Like and own your reason for choosing it, as there can be a lot of healing there. This can be a form of acceptance because you are no longer feeling disempowered by your situation but rather empowered by your choice.

Digital Devices and Boundaries

One day I received a text message that sent me into a negative spiral. After I held compassion for myself, gave attention to my feelings, and recharged, I was ready to engage and respond. This was a process I adopted as I was going through my self-care journey, and it helped immensely with my stress, anxiety, and energy levels. Anytime I tell clients they get to decide how and when they want to respond to texts, emails, voicemails, etc., they are always relieved. "Oh, I can do that? This is great!" they tell me. It's almost like they were waiting for permission for someone to tell them they could even consider the idea. Once I offer that to my clients, it's amazing how all these new boundaries pop up.

There is a lot of pressure in the digital age for instant response time, and instant gratification. But here's a secret: You can make up your own rules. Have you heard of business owners who have completely sworn off email? I have met a few, and they literally do not use email. I aspire to that one day. I'm not a huge fan of email, except the ones I like to read. Mainly, I hate the pressure to respond.

It gives me anxiety when Gmail tells me, "It's been seven days, send a reply?" My heart sinks and I'm like, "Oh crap . . ." Then my brain loops in thoughts of how I'm a bad person for not responding sooner, and what will they think of me? So, if you email me, you may or may not get a response, but know that I will read it! I LOVE emails from my readers.

You don't have to do things the way others do. Even if the rest of the world is responding instantaneously, you get to decide how you want to respond and interact with the world. But what about work? I can't decide there. They decide for me. For work engagements, create a mutual response time agreement that works for both parties. If the company has a specific communication policy, that's fine during working hours, but then outside work hours, you make your own rules. I find that most of my clients adhere to their work communication rules even during off hours, which throws off their work/life balance. Separate your company's work communication policy from yours. What will be your personal communication policy?

Notice when digital devices or your relationship to the digital world triggers your stress, anxiety, depression, etc. The digital devices alone don't cause stress, but rather your thoughts about how you should behave and feel. Give yourself permission to engage with the world in a way that is nurturing and aligned for you.

Once you create a boundary for yourself about how you want to engage with the world, you will experience more peace. When do you want to check your messages? When do you want to respond? Make an agreement with yourself. How do you want to engage with life? What is the life you want to live?

Journal and Reflection Questions

1. How do I feel after using my phone?
2. How do I feel after being on social media?
3. How do I feel when I get a text or email?
4. Do I feel pressured to respond? Why or why not?
5. How do I want to feel with my digital devices?
6. How much time do I want to take off from them?
7. How do I want to respond when someone messages me?
8. When do I want to respond when someone messages me?
9. What do I want to use digital devices for?

10. What do I not want to use digital devices for?

11. What is my personal communication policy?

12. What do I want my personal communication policy to be?

How to Create a Self-Care Practice

Next we are going to use the three parts of engaging to help you create a self-care plan and practice.

Make a decision: This step is where you make your self-care plan. Based on what you uncovered in the foundations and earlier exercises, what did you learn about yourself?

What do you want to gain out of practicing self-care? What will help you achieve that? What would you like your self-care practice to look like? How do you want to feel? What activities do you want to commit to? How many minutes a day/week will you commit to? What will you do during that time? How will you use your self-care plan?

Make space: How can you make room for your decision—in your mind, in your physical space/life, and in your spirit? What will you have to change, modify, or swap in order to have space to execute? At what time of the day will you do this, or have it completed by? How and where will you schedule it into your current life? How can you make this easier to make it happen? (i.e., have clothes ready, chop veggies the night before).

Take action: How will you execute your self-care plan? How will you be accountable to yourself? How will you measure your progress? What resistance are you facing? What are some tools to keep handy to help you work through your resistance? How will you reward yourself? Maybe every time you take the action, you drop a marble in a jar. And when you reach a certain number of marbles, you can purchase new headphones, treat yourself out, or simply gift yourself a two-hour break from life, or enjoy the sunset.

Here's an example of a simple self-care plan:

- **Decision**: I want to focus on my mental and physical well-being. For that, I will walk every day for twenty-minutes. I want to feel more energy, detox from the day, and build stamina.
- **Space**: I am walking before lunch. I have my clothes, shoes, headphones, and phone ready and available to make it easier.
- **Action**: By 11:00 a.m. every day I have my clothes and materials prepared so it's easy to change and I go on my walk!

Blocks to Caring for Yourself

As you are developing a self-care plan and working on building these new habits, notice where you are blocking yourself from care. Notice where you are giving reasons not to care for yourself. Maybe you're telling yourself reasons why it won't work.

Your Own Inner Limitations

These will come in all forms. It may come from thinking you don't have the resources, or that you don't deserve it, or from an outside idea that you adopted about it being silly. Separate what is story or fact in your head. Is this idea really true? Is it a fact? Or did someone tell you this?

Here are a few common thinking patterns that may block us from caring for ourselves:

"I'm being selfish."
"I feel guilty."
"What will people think?"

Notice where you don't feel good about doing something for yourself. Or where you don't allow yourself to do something because of one of the above reasons. The reason may be valid, or it may not be; it is up to you to decipher that. Most importantly, you want to like your reason for choosing what you choose. Choosing consciously is an act of self-care.

Lack of Resources

We can never have a lack of resources to care for ourselves because we technically don't need anything but our own attention. Yet our brains like to tell us that we are lacking certain things, so let's address them.

"I don't have time." We could all use more time in the day. But ultimately the time we have is the time we have, and we get to choose where and how we spend it. If you prefer to spend all your time on someone and something else, do what feels right for you. But if your heart has been aching for more time, then you ought to create time for yourself.

This might mean borrowing time from somewhere else or becoming more efficient in other tasks. It will require your creativity. What I also know is that when we truly desire something and move toward it, the universe meets us halfway.

What you seek is seeking you too.

RUMI

I have seen this to be true countless number of times. I remember a time I was working in management consulting, and I really wanted to do the Strengths Finder test. My mentor had told me about it, and I wanted to understand myself more through it. My schedule was extremely packed. I was involved in multiple activities at work and outside of work, and I hadn't gotten to it yet.

One day I walked into work for a Woman's Day at work, and there was a book titled *Strength Finders* on each chair. A certified consultant did an entire workshop with us, we got time to do the test AT work, and each person there got a free copy of the book. It was something on my heart that I wanted to do, and although I hadn't gotten to it yet, the universe inserted it into my life and made it happen. You'll be surprised how these things magically happen. And when they do, send me your stories because I truly delight in them!

"I don't have money," or "It's too expensive." Self-care absolutely does not need to cost any money! Self-care is about tuning into your needs and honoring them. How can you focus on comforting yourself in a way that doesn't cost money?

Also notice the money ideas that come up for you and separate fact from story. Ask yourself questions to explore alternatives. Get creative with it. Is it true that it's really expensive? Or is this something you value and would be proud to spend your money on? Or is there an alternative but cheaper option? Is there something else you can do that would feel just as good?

I remember many, many times I needed a self-care day and did not have much money at all. I loved taking myself out to dinner, but that wasn't always in the budget. So, I had to get creative unless I wanted to lose my mind being indoors all day.

When I lived in California, I would take a drive to the beach, park, or lake near me. At the beach I loved just watching the waves crash and sometimes people-watch the surfers out in the sea. Sometimes I would simply sit on a bench at the park and leave my phone in the car. There were also times when I went to the Tuesday dollar movie screenings as a way to unwind and detox from the day.

When I lived in Chicago, I used to love driving along Lakeshore Drive. I found it so therapeutic, even more so when someone else drove, and I could simply stare out the window at Lake Michigan.

Notice for yourself where you are denying yourself self-care because of a lack of resources, whatever that may be. Remind yourself that no resource is truly needed but yourself. And allow yourself to think creatively and out of the box on what you could do, or be, to practice care for yourself today.

Bringing in Your Self-Care Skills

As you are continuing your self-care journey, if you hit any roadblocks, you want to come back to the self-care skills we talked about in Part One. As you grow, there will be new challenges that show up, and these skills will come in handy once again.

Those skills are: courage, confidence, introspection, and execution.

Courage: There will be moments that you will have to have the courage to stand alone or against the grain to honor your self-care.

Confidence: There will be moments you will have to conquer your self-doubt and have the confidence to speak up to someone in order to practice your self-care.

Introspection: When you are overwhelmed with emotion or stress, turning inward will be an especially helpful skill to help you uncover what's going on so you can take aligned action.

Execution: Sometimes we have everything we need to move forward but still are not able to execute. How can you focus on taking action? Often introspection will help with this.

Start Small

You don't have to change your entire life and turn it upside down to start your self-care practice. You can start right here, right now. Don't worry about doing it right; just focus on starting. The best way to start is by starting small. Your self-care plan can be as little as a simple five-minute practice once a week. I invite you to start there if you feel overwhelmed at the idea of starting. Start with once a week and keep adding a day until you're at seven days in a row. Small wins and small progress lead to big wins and big progress.

If you've started small and are ready for a bigger leap into self-care, join me in Chapter 9, where we will create your self-care road map for the next one hundred days.

The main question to ask: What's one step I can take right now that is aligned to my self-care needs?

> *Let what wants to come, come.*
> *Let what wants to go, go*
> *If it is mine, it will stay.*
> *If not, whatever is better will replace it.*
> TOSHA SILVER

PART THREE

Flow

Burnout Recovery and Creating Work/Life Balance

Don't get so busy making a living that you forget to make a life.
Dolly Parton

A manager at one of my consulting gigs didn't respond to emails after 5:00 p.m. I was told this by a team member so I would know when I'd be able to reach her. I was pretty impressed and asked "How so?" My peer told me that she spends her evenings with her kids, and that is her cut-off time until the next morning. I wondered why more people didn't do that. The work culture there was that most people worked whatever hours they were needed. I could see how many people were miserable because of it. But they didn't think they could do anything else. So then, how did this manager pull it off?

I realized that work-life balance comes from us and is created by us. It takes courage to take charge of your life, to decide what you want, and to do what you need to make it happen. Though some people frowned upon this manager's boundary, she held firm with it. She was a great manager who was an asset to the company and always delivered her work on time, so they respected it. I felt so inspired by her example.

Companies are now slowly starting to take initiative around wellbeing and work/life balance, but there is a long road ahead of us. You, as an individual, should feel empowered to decide and create what you want. Maybe you won't be able to do or get to everything on your list, but even one small tweak can do wonders for your well-being. We cannot rely on top leadership to do it for us, because when you look closely, often they are burned out themselves and do not have a work/life balance. A major culture shift is needed on all levels from the top down.

Deloitte recently released a well-being report that showed that 70 percent of executives in the workplace want to switch jobs for greater well-being. This is important to note. Many people are struggling with well-being at all levels of companies, and now we have an opportunity to create a new baseline. And it starts with us.

Deloitte's report said, "One out of three employees and executives are constantly struggling with fatigue and poor mental health. . . . As we've seen with the Great Resignation, many people are no longer willing to tolerate jobs that leave them unhappy and in a constant state of stress and fatigue."[5]

Some interesting facts:

- Work is among the top three sources of stress for Americans.
- US businesses lose up to $300 billion yearly as a result of workplace stress.
- Stress causes around one million workers to miss work every day.
- Only 43 percent of US employees think their employers care about their work/life balance.
- Work-related stress causes 120,000 deaths[6] and results in $190 billion in healthcare costs yearly.[7]

I'm writing this chapter during a year in which I burned out three times. Yes, three times. This experience reminded me that stress isn't something we can always avoid, but it is something we can learn to navigate. This was the first time in my life where I burned out and actually had tools to move through it. This is a miracle in itself. In the past, I had been left with extra weight on my body, hair loss, pimples, and tears as I sobbed through my misery. This time I still had some of that, but I had a much better way to hold myself through it. Moving through those three periods showed me the power of this work and how things can shift quite rapidly with dedication and focus.

What Is Work/Life Balance?

Work/life balance is a big topic in today's world. Everyone is trying to figure it out. Some people have found their sweet spot, others are navigating their way to it, and yet others don't believe it's possible or have given up on it completely! And yet others are going with the ebb and flow of life and creating unique work/life balance scenarios as their life fluctuates.

Finding balance is about devoting your time to each part of your personal and professional life in a way that feels right for you. This includes managing your time, energy, space, and feelings of fulfillment. There is no direct definition of finding balance. You get to decide what that means for you. Ask yourself, "What does it feel like to feel balanced? When do I feel balanced? How can I create more balance?"

Here's the tricky part: No one can figure this out for you. This is your opportunity to figure out. The reason is that work/life balance is not a plug-and-play technique. It is a unique formula that will be uncovered through discovery. The only way to find your sweet spot is through trial and error.

Think of it like an unfolding. Consider it a fun project or assignment that you have been given. The reward of it is your life. You have more time, more energy, and more joy as you uncover this formula for yourself.

In this next section I'm going to share with you my burnout story, how I recovered, and the steps I took to create my own work/life balance. As you read, notice any themes that resonate with you, or that you notice in your own life. Then I will walk you through the steps you can use for your own burnout recovery and balance.

My Burnout Recovery Story

How it happened . . .

There are many reasons for the burnout I experienced during that twelve-month period. It was a mix of personal and work components. My clients quadrupled, and I did not have the organizational structure or self-care plan in place for that increase in workload. I went from having one hundred clients over multiple years to having one hundred new clients in nine months! I was so excited to work with these clients that I took on way more than my body's capacity could actually handle. And truly, I had no idea what my threshold was at the time.

Everyone around me was working just as much as me, so I figured it was normal. Working is often valued by society, and it can have an addictive quality to it. My workaholic tendencies kicked in for multiple reasons: I enjoyed my work, it made me feel important, and it allowed me to avoid things in my own life I didn't want to deal with. My people-pleaser tendencies made it worse because I didn't always know how to say no or was afraid of getting in trouble.

Having more clients is a good problem to have, but combined with other personal struggles, it became too overwhelming all at once. There were some old wounds I was working on healing, but I had no idea how painful it would be once I opened that can of worms. The work stress on top of the personal stress completely turned my health upside down.

Over a period of three months, I gained fifteen pounds, had multiple meltdowns, and for many weeks was barely floating above water. I was in survival mode just trying to make it to the next day. It wasn't easy, but I'm so dang proud of myself for holding myself through it all. I am now writing to you from the other side. Here's how the three burnouts happened.

Burnout #1

When I got the first wave of new clients, I was so excited and was working around the clock. I had prayed for this. It was happening. I wanted to work with everyone and do all the things I could to help them. I was going faster than my body could handle. In about six weeks I completely crashed.

That week I saw sixteen clients in three days. By the end of the third day, my brain was completely mush. I thought I could sleep it off, but the next morning my brain was in a complete fog. I could not think straight. I could barely do any tasks. It felt like carrying a 100-pound weight just to send one text or email out to a client.

In a team meeting, I could barely gather what people were saying. It was going right over my head as if they were speaking a foreign language. That's when I realized something was off.

That weekend I had a solo trip planned to Washington, DC. I decided this had to be a self-care trip because I had no energy for my original plans. I needed a getaway more than ever.

Once I checked into my hotel room in DC, I found myself in pain. I had a urinary tract infection. This is when my inner 911 alarm officially went off. Not only was I in extreme exhaustion and brain fog, but my body also now had an infection! This is when I truly realized I was burned out and something needed to change—ASAP!

Burnout #2

This happened a few months later as my personal struggles started to spring up. After receiving a few difficult comments from people in my life, I went into a negative spiral. It brought to surface a lot of trauma from my past, and it led to a complete meltdown.

The following two weeks were horrible. I felt extremely down. I thought this would be the end of it and it would pass, but it got worse. For a total of about six weeks, it felt like I was in a complete hell hole. Things just kept happening.

It was really hard to balance work while I was dying inside emotionally. I felt exhausted physically and emotionally. I wasn't sure how I was going to make it through to the end of the year.

Burnout #3

After that six-week stint, my body crashed, and I got super sick. I had a full week off from work and was excited to go on a short road trip, but those plans went out the window. Instead, I spent it blowing my nose, rubbing Vicks on my forehead, and weeping in bed. My body completely shut down from all the intensity of the previous six weeks.

This was burnout #3. I completely surrendered. I had no other choice. I was in bed unable to work, think, or do anything. I had a runny nose, fever, and cough. This sickness came and went and continued for almost three weeks.

It forced me to really be patient with myself, kind with myself, and really tune into what was going on inside me. I really wanted to get better and get on with my life, but my body didn't feel the same way. Many of my plans got canceled, and I was forced to rest.

How I Handled It

When I hit the burnout #1, I started at Step 3 of the CARE Formula: recharge. I cared for myself before anything else. I rested and slowly brought my energy levels back up. Once I was feeling better mentally and physically, I moved back into Step 2: Paying attention. I decided to lean in and take a closer look, to connect with myself deeper to understand what was going on.

I asked myself questions like:

- Which days do I feel the most burned out?
- What tasks do I find really draining?
- How can I make this easier for myself?

I thought about these questions, and I also wrote some things down to help me investigate deeper. Through these questions I was able to discover a few things. There were certain tasks I absolutely hated doing that drained my energy more. I also wasn't taking proper breaks between client calls. I sometimes would sit for a straight six to eight hours with back-to-back clients on Zoom, other meetings, and tasks. I also realized I was not nourishing and cleansing myself at all with the amount of emotional heaviness I was taking in from these clients.

These were a few insights that helped me move into Step 4: Engage. I wanted to create a new way of doing things to help prevent me from experiencing burnout again. I made a list of things to do.

I started taking breaks.

Since then, I've been a lot more diligent about taking breaks. Even if I only have three minutes between one call to the next, I am more likely now to go outside on the back patio and soak in some sun. If I have to use the restroom when the next client joins, I ask them if they don't mind if I use the restroom quickly, rather than holding it in the whole time, which I have done before (omg, the agony).

I became more efficient with tasks I hated.

I could see where I was spending way too much time on client notes and decided to become briefer and only write the major important points rather than record everything. I also became more disciplined about completing those tasks within twenty-four hours, or at the latest within the week. Before I was letting those tasks pile up for weeks, which made it even harder to catch up. After that, I was barely ever behind on this specific task again, and if I was one or two times, I would catch it and make sure to finish it that week rather than letting it linger for weeks.

I stopped working on my off days.

Because I was so excited about the work I was doing and this new influx of clients, I always wanted to work. I was ON a LOT of the time. I was checking my work email and texts on my off hours and days. I was responding to messages at all hours of the night. I could tell I was getting addicted at one point because I would check my work inbox multiple times, even though there were no new notifications. That's when I realized there was a problem here.

After some digging, I realized that this work made me feel important and that I was needed. The desire for this feeling was causing me to be more present at work and not in a good way. I was overly present to the point where there were NO tasks/messages waiting for me. This was leading me to burnout!

I decided I had to become stricter about my hours, and when I was off, I had to TRULY take off. I almost had to force myself.

I started setting boundaries.

I realized my work was starting to come at the cost of my health. This is where boundaries came in. If someone asked me to take over a project or a client, I didn't say yes right away. I stepped back to tune into my energy levels and to also see if this was truly in alignment with what I wanted to take on. I started being pickier with how I spent my time.

I stopped feeling bad if my client was waiting to hear back from me. I had always been upfront with my clients about my response time, yet I still would respond earlier than that. I decided to start honoring the timeframes I had said and gave myself more space to respond. I reminded myself that no one was going to die if I didn't respond by a certain time. If there was truly an emergency, they can call 911 or someone else.

I started speaking up.

When I initially burnt out, I said nothing. I felt embarrassed, like a fraud, and a loser. But after a few weeks of settling into this realization that I burned out and had set a few practices in place, I started to speak out.

I shared with a few colleagues that I had burned out a few weeks ago. They all listened and commended me for being vulnerable with them. Many of them expressed that they knew what it felt like, and they invited me to have grace with myself and to ask for support if I needed it. I was super grateful, and I felt so much better after releasing some of the shame around it by talking about it with others.

I adjusted my schedule.

The way my schedule was set up was a sure set up for burnout. I was seeing way too many clients in a short period of time. I decided to spread out certain client sessions with a two-day break in between so it wasn't back-to-back.

Since I was such an eager beaver to work with all these clients, I did not take into account the emotional toll that would come from seeing so many people back-to-back. I realized this wasn't sustainable.

Work Burnout versus Personal Burnout

When burnout #2 and #3 came, they were really more wrapped around my personal struggles. This required a bit of a different strategy. This experience invited me to lean in deeper to my internal pain, speak to my hurting inner child, and have extreme compassion and patience with myself.

It wasn't easy. Those six to eight weeks were one of the hardest times of that year. After a ton of struggles, I came to a point where I decided I was going to take better care of myself to help me through it.

My self-care plan included walking, drinking more water, and saying one kind thing to myself each day. All of this helped a lot. The walking is what I was most consistent with, and it truly helped me clear my head and process the heavy emotions I was feeling.

All three burnouts that year helped me better myself personally and professionally. I am very proud of how I handled them, even though I felt immense shame when the first one happened. I also realized going through these experiences just meant more content for my book!

This also helped me truly walk my talk and practice the tools I am sharing with you here. So now that you've gotten to walk through my burnout and recovery with me, let's talk about your burnout recovery and work/life balance.

How to Recover from Burnout

Once you've hit burnout, the very first thing you must do is up your self-care, mentally and emotionally. What do I mean by UP your self-care? First, decide that this is your priority. Create space for it. And make the decisions and actions to make it happen. Yes, I know it's easier said than done, but that is the path to start with. Ask yourself the questions below.

And you might tell me, "I don't have time for all these questions! I need to recover from my burnout now and I need something quick." I got something for you. Skip down to: 3 steps to burnout recovery.

Journal and Reflection Questions

1. What is important to me?
2. What do I value?
3. What is my priority?
4. Is self-care my priority? Why or why not?
5. How can I make self-care my priority?
6. What does self-care for me look like?
7. What do I really need right now?

Three Steps to Burnout Recovery

1. Recharge. First things first, you must rest. Focus on sleep, having down time, and staying low key with plans. Recharging will look different for everyone. Refer to the recharge activities list in Chapter 7.

Ask yourself, "How can I recharge and rest right now? What do I really need right now?"

Sometimes the answer might even be: "I really need a hug right now." Go ahead and give yourself one. When you are burned out there is sometimes a part of you that wants to be acknowledged, seen, and comforted. You can be that person for yourself and if there's someone you feel comfortable with, get a hug from them, and allow yourself to be seen, even in conversation.

If you have a schedule with long working hours making it difficult to do a recharge, see how you can nurture yourself more during the hours that you are off, whatever that might be.

2. Reflect. As you recharge you will start to gain some energy. Initially there is no space to reflect because you are just so tired. I've been there. And I remember thinking, *Reflecting isn't working right now; I need to rest first.* And after I did, I would get ideas later. Ask yourself, "Where am I feeling burned out? Is it at work? Is it at home? Or somewhere else?"

Keep asking questions to understand more about your burnout. "How does burnout affect me? What do I want to have/be/feel instead?" Then ask yourself what your ideal situation would be and consider three potential possibilities, and three unrealistic ones.

3. Redirect. As you recharge and reflect, you'll have some ideas and insights on what you want to do or experiment with.

I remember feeling burned out from having Zoom video calls on multiple days of the week. I wondered if I could condense these calls to only two days instead. So, I adjusted my calendar and tested it out, and it made a huge difference for me. To have more open days of rest and working on my own hours without any calls made me feel so productive. I still got my work done. Plus, I had all this spacious time. Though I will say that on those two days I often felt very exhausted, so I would nurture myself extra on those days and take more breaks.

Creating Your Work/Life Balance

Building and practicing this will be your key to preventing burnout. Remember, that this will be unique to you, so don't worry about what your neighbor, coworker, or sister is doing. Work/life balance is a very personal journey and choice. What is balanced for you may be chaotic for someone else and vice versa.

To determine your own balance, you will want to look at your own life, your personal needs, and unique desires. This may feel uncomfortable because we are often looking for a handout or manual on how to do xyz. I will give you some steps, but ultimately the roadmap is yours to create.

You want to uncover your working threshold. How many hours of the day are you sharp and at your most productive? After how many hours do you have to stop before you start going into depletion? Usually by this time you are cranky or snappy and possibly just want to get home.

Three Steps to Work/Life Balance

1. Determine your own work/life balance.

First, you have to look at what currently is. If you were to rate your work/life balance from 1-10, with 10 being balanced, and 1 not so much, what would you give it? Then ask yourself why. Write out the pros and cons of each thing. Dig deeper, ask more questions.

Then ask yourself, "In an ideal world, what would my work/life balance be if I had all the resources and time possible?" Don't worry about if it can happen, or at least not yet. Just allow yourself to bring it to life in your mind.

How do you want your life to look, feel, and be? How do you want your work to look, feel, and be? What matters most to you? Where do you want to spend your time? You are connecting to your own personal truth and desires. To create work/life balance, you have to first decide what that means to you and what that looks like.

2. Stay open to possibility.

When you first think about your ideal situation, you are probably going to reject half of it. You will think it's not possible. You will think you are being unrealistic. You will think you are silly for even doing this. But when you start thinking of possible ideas, you'll be surprised at how sometimes it starts to happen on its own. Perhaps you had been thinking of taking off on Fridays, and the next week your company announced Friday Free day, where the entire company is off on every third Friday of every month. My friend told me her company offers this as a perk. I thought that was pretty cool! I get excited to see how companies are creating more well-being and recharge initiatives for staff.

To create possibility, you are going to create a list of ideas and possibilities of how it might be attainable. Make a list of ten things that could be possible. And make a list of ten things that are totally unrealistic, but you dream of how it may be possible. If you can't do the full activity right now, just think of one in your head for both. You'll be surprised how something from that unrealistic list actually happens. Stay open to the possibilities.

You can decide that something is possible, even if you don't know how or what yet. Allow yourself to think bigger. And if you have a hard time, play this game with yourself to make it more fun and loosen up your brain. To help you think bigger on what is possible, you can try saying, "In a wacky world, this could totally happen because of xyz."

For example, if you don't believe you'd be able to stop working at 4:00 p.m. because the shop where you work closes at 7:00 p.m., you can say, "In a wacky world, I could totally stop working at 4:00 p.m. if my boss started closing the shop at

4:00 p.m." And if you can't find a reason, just say, "In a wacky world, I'd totally be able to work nine months a year and take off the other three months and travel." Imagine that you are in a land of possibility where the options are endless. You might be surprised by what actually might happen if you dare to dream.

3. Start one thing tomorrow.

Sometimes with planning, we get lost in it. So I recommend that you definitely think about and create a long-term plan after deciding what you want. But until then, I invite you to pick just one thing you're going to start doing tomorrow, right away.

I'm going to tell you to start immediately tomorrow. What is one thing you can put into place now? It can be something that takes as little as five minutes or even one minute!

Put it in your calendar, set an alarm on your phone, and make it happen. Remind yourself why this is important for you. And commit to creating your work/life balance and self-care routine.

When I started having a bigger client load, I found myself at the computer a lot. I would be sitting for hours, and I could tell how tense my body felt, and how cramped my energy felt. But work had to get done! So I just pushed through and crashed later. I realized something had to change because I was feeling crazy from being in one room all day and on a computer, often on video calls.

The one small thing I started implementing right away was going outside in between my calls. Often in between my calls, I would just stay on the computer and complete another task. But this made the continued computer time feel exhausting. Then I noticed, even if I only had three minutes before my next call, I would jump up to get my outside time.

It was fun to see that shift because my tendency is to just continue and do another task. There was a study done by Microsoft that showed three things: 1) "Breaks between [Zoom] meetings allow the brain to 'reset,' reducing a cumulative buildup of stress across meetings"; 2) "Back-to-back meetings can decrease your ability to focus and engage"; and 3) "Transitioning between meetings can be a source of high stress." This study proves that short breaks of even just ten minutes can make a huge difference in focus and stress levels.[8]

What is one small thing you can start tomorrow? Just pick one and start it. Even something as little as sixty seconds will help!

Most importantly, I want you to know this isn't some dream vision board you are creating hoping it comes to life. It is possible to have energy, fulfillment, and balance in a way that feels good for you. You are actively creating and living these solutions. Being on the other side of these three burnouts, I can truly say that it IS working.

I have colleagues that are complaining about burnout, and I have been able to share with them my stories from this year and give them many tips. Many of them have reached out to me to tell me which tip they implemented and how it has helped them.

It gives me so much joy to know that people can enjoy their lives and not be trapped by their work. Life is meant to be lived, not worked. I'd love to hear what worked for you. Feel free to share your stories with me by emailing me or tagging me on social media. All my contact info is at the back of this book. I can't wait to read your stories.

Work Boundaries

Her phone was blowing up after work hours. Her boss and other vendors kept pinging her with work requests. She felt a need to be on her phone constantly to respond, and it was interrupting her family time.

This client shared with me during our coaching call how these messages were stressing her out and was really affecting her home life. I asked her if these messages were truly urgent, or if they could they?

She said they could definitely wait. I asked her why she felt the need to respond if they could wait. Because she was in such a GO mode, she hadn't even considered the idea. She just felt the urge to GO and respond.

I know many of us do this and feel the same way. We are so used to being ON that we have no idea how to turn off, how to recharge. And often we don't realize we have the choice to turn off or not respond at the moment because we worry about what someone will think if we don't respond, or we worry about missing the mark or messing up.

After we moved through the reasons, she made a decision about when her time off from work would be, and the boundary she would set on when she would respond to messages. I asked her if she ever used airplane mode to turn off from all the noise. This way you literally don't have to see or receive messages until you are ready to. She paused and thought about it and said she had never even thought of that. "What a great idea," she told me.

She decided to create boundaries around when she was available for work, when she'd respond to messages, and what mode of communication was best for her (email versus text). Till then she was giving her power away to whoever was reaching out to her, creating panic and anxiety in her feeling the need to respond. Now, by deciding her parameters, she was able to have real time to recharge rather than letting the world dictate to her when she gets to rest.

In a world of constant GO, it is hard to turn off when people can reach us at all hours of the day with all sorts of different mediums like text, call, social media, and more. It leaves no space for downtime unless you create it yourself.

Turn Down Routine

When I stayed in Tulum, Mexico, I was offered a turn down service. I had no idea what this meant but I was intrigued. To help you wind down for the day, they spray essential oils in your hotel room and bring hot tea between the hours of 6:00 and 8:00 p.m. I thought it was a wonderful concept! I loved it! I had never experienced a turn down service before.

It made me think about how we can have a turn down routine for after a workday. There were many times I stopped working, but I was still wired. I felt kind of crazy, like I needed to be doing something. I felt a bit frantic, even though I tried to sit down and chill.

I realized I needed a transition activity to help me calm down and relax.

A few ideas to help you create your own turn down routine: using essential oils, taking a bath, napping for twenty-minutes, walking outside for ten minutes, sitting down and sipping tea, listening to a podcast, going for a short drive, using salts in the shower, play with the dog, painting your nails, foot spa, window shopping, playing a game . . . the possibilities are endless.

Your turn down routine can literally change every day, but having a few ideas handy can give you some to choose from! I often turn down in different ways, but they are usually a mixture of a few things. I'd say a bath and essential oils are my favorite. When I have long days with clients, sometimes I am wiped out, and lying in the tub for twenty minutes really rejuvenates me. What helps you transition from on to off?

CHAPTER **10**

Special Topics of Care: Depression, Anxiety, Bullying, and More

Your pain is not your personality.
KEVIN BREEL

Growing up in America as a person of color, I got bullied a lot for my culture, skin color, and other traits. I didn't feel accepted in America, and when I traveled to India to visit family, I felt different there too. By Americans, I was considered Indian, and by Indians, I was considered American. It made me feel like neither accepted me as their own. I felt unwanted as though I didn't belong. It was difficult for a young mind to absorb. I experienced more bullying for other things all the way through college. Then, in my adult years, I faced the deepest depression of my life and learned I had massive anxiety, both of which affected me deeply.

This chapter is dedicated to special focused areas of care. We are going to talk about stress that arises around topics including holidays, bullying, hate crimes, depression, anxiety, family, suicidal ideation, and more.

Holiday Stress

Why are the holidays so stressful? I cannot speak for how it is in the rest of the world, but I can speak from what I've seen growing up in America. People stress about decor, trees, presents, the people they don't want to see, the parties they don't want to attend, as well as the parties they are hosting. Often it feels like a big ball of overwhelm, and sometimes a very unpleasant experience.

One of the most profound things I learned from some peers in the mental health space is that you get to create the kind of holiday you want for you.

Don't want to participate in gift giving, even though everyone around you is? Then don't. Rather travel than sit around in someone's living room? Decide where you will go. Have no interest in decorating this year? Do something else instead.

You might tell me it's not possible. Your family wouldn't be OKAY with it. Or this is your family tradition. I'm not telling you to change anything if you don't want to. But if you're not enjoying your holidays, think about how much stress you are causing yourself by doing things you don't want to do. Consider what you truly want to do rather than what the customs and traditions say or what has always been done. You can break the mold.

If you cannot make a grand change because of logistics or multiple decision makers that are involved, then instead think about one little tweak that would make you jump for the moon. How can you bring joy to your holiday experience? Example: Maybe you hate wrapping gifts, so instead you get them professionally wrapped at the mall! Maybe you don't want to attend the company holiday party, so instead you skip out and spend the evening with someone special in your life. One small tweak!

You will be much happier spending the holidays the way you want.

Journal and Reflection Questions
1. What feels stressful about the holidays?
2. How do I want to feel during the holidays?
3. What do I want to do and not want do during the holidays?
4. What matters to me during the holidays?
5. How can I create more of that?

Travel Stress

When I lived and worked in Tulum, Mexico, for a month, I got kicked out of my Airbnb because the electricity went out. They moved my reservation to a new Airbnb, but I had to get there myself after dark. I couldn't find a cab to go to my new accommodation. I was beyond stressed.

When I eventually got to my new Airbnb, I couldn't get in. The lockbox key was not working. I tried calling Airbnb, the security guard did not speak English, no one was able to help me. I finally surrendered and plopped on the stairs with all my things and cried my eyes out. I felt helpless and didn't know what to do. Some neighbors saw me and came to help. Luckily, they were able to get me inside.

When you are traveling, there are so many unknowns and surprises. Make sure to take extra gentle care of yourself as you are navigating all the ups and downs that come with it. I definitely learned some lessons after that experience to make future travel less stressful!

Another helpful thing with travel stress is to notice what about travel is stressing you out. Is it the packing part? Is it the flying part? See if you can find ways to make the process easier for yourself and make a travel self-care routine for yourself.

I found packing to be stressful, so I've implemented a few things to help me reduce the stress. For example, I will make an agreement with myself to have my bag packed the night before, rather than doing it the morning of, which I have done before (it was a nightmare). I also try to get all my errands done forty-eight hours before, because I've been that person running around the last day, having to shop AND pack. It's just too much. How can you make your travel a bit smoother?

Journal and Reflection Questions
1. What feels stressful about traveling?
2. What would make traveling easier if anything were possible?
3. How can I create some of that?
4. What can you do earlier to be better prepared?

Family Stress

They say you can take the most spiritual person in the room, place them with their family, and all that wisdom disappears. So many people struggle with family stress. Either they cannot stand certain family members, are traumatized by the way they've been treated, don't feel true love and safety, or something else.

One holiday I felt overwhelmed by an interaction I'd had with someone and couldn't sleep all night. The next day, there was a group gathering, and I still felt angry and charged up. I felt that if anyone rubbed me the wrong way, I might say something I'd regret.

I decided I wanted to calm down because I didn't want to make a scene, and I wanted to enjoy this holiday. I had come back to visit and hadn't seen many people in years. I was looking forward to it until this interaction happened the night before. Then I started to dread it.

I worked the CARE method we learned in Chapter 4. First, I held compassion for myself and validated my feelings. I reminded myself that it was okay to feel hurt and upset so I could let the emotions flow through me. Then I paid attention to how I was feeling, I journaled, asked questions, and went deeper into why I felt the way I did. Third,

I decided to recharge. When everyone else was hanging out before the gathering, I decided to spend quiet alone time to reset myself.

After recharging, I reflected on what was important to me. I decided it was to enjoy the holiday. I focused on this intention and thought about how I could do that. I redirected my energy. I decided ahead of time how I would respond if someone said something to me. Fourth, it was time to engage. I ended up heading to the event with a family member I was close to and spoke my feelings out, maybe even cried a little. I felt supported and went into the event feeling better and focused on enjoying myself. I enjoyed the decor, the smell of the apple pie, the beautiful layout of the food, and the spirit of the holiday.

The point I want to share here is that you can turn your experience into what you want it to be. No, we cannot control the situation or the people, but we can decide what matters, who we want to engage with, and what we will and will not tolerate that evening, and politely exit if necessary.

Bullying, Racism, Abuse, Sexism, Hate Crimes, and More

Experiencing any form of abuse, violence, or hate can be damaging for life. Whether it happened many years ago and is a traumatic memory or is an ongoing reality, it requires deep, deep care for yourself. This can look like many things, but a few examples are giving yourself grace, holding compassionate space for yourself, loving on yourself, holding yourself through the pain, speaking kindly to yourself, joining a support group, talking to a friend, creating a boundary, having a difficult conversation, or more.

It is important to surround yourself with community, people who love you, or even strangers you can connect with. The trauma that comes up from any of these scenarios is important to acknowledge in order to care for yourself. Heavy emotions need space to breathe. Creating safe space to process, reflect, and connect with yourself and others can be a powerful practice.

It can be very scary and even traumatic to face the pain. If you are open to working with someone you trust, a mentor, a coach, or a therapist, it will be helpful. Even having a friend or stranger to listen to your story can be incredibly healing.

Self-expression is another way to care for yourself through processing the pain. Some people write poems, write songs, make videos or art to help process the emotions. I have found that writing a letter to my past self or to the people involved (even if I never send it) has been very helpful.

Journal and Reflection Questions
1. Who do I feel safe to talk to about this?
2. What groups can I join for community support?
3. Where am I hurting inside?
4. How can I nurture myself more?

Depression

Having experienced depression for many years, I know it's not easy to live with. The heaviness you carry in your body every single day. Not wanting to talk to or face anyone. It's the worst. And no one gets it unless they get it. It can be a very lonely and isolating experience.

I never knew I was depressed until my late twenties. That is when it hit me hard like a ton of bricks. Almost like all the pain I had carried in my body for over twenty years came bursting out of a shell that was hiding inside me. The catalyst was a heartbreak that turned into a very heavy depression for two years. I used to be a social butterfly, but I had stopped talking to almost everyone in my life and turned inward.

What I have discovered through the years is that depression is trying to tell us something. It has a message for us. Though it might feel like a dead end, I don't think it is. I think the depression is actually leading us to our freedom if we are daring enough to dig deeper.

Debilitating Depression

When you are feeling debilitating depression and can barely get out of bed, during those times you may not have the energy to explore anything. So, at that point you want to focus on the basics. Do any one small thing that you can do, to take care of yourself. That might be using the restroom when you need to, maybe washing your face, or simply getting out of bed regardless of what time it is.

Sometimes, these small wins can be everything. Acknowledge the small steps. Provide yourself a safe space to allow yourself to be depressed instead of resisting it. Take care of your depression. Love on it, even if you don't understand it.

Whenever I was in this space, I learned to stop judging myself for it. Instead, I would see how I could nurture my spirit. It can feel hopeless and defeating to be depressed. But instead, if you allow it, it will let the depression move through you rather than getting trapped. I have found this to be one of the most helpful tips, to allow and focus on simple things you can do to care for yourself.

Functional Depression

When you are in functional depression, this is where you can find some space to explore. Maybe you have to go to work, or you have errands you need to do. You are depressed, but you are also functioning in everyday life. There would be a time when I would be functional in the day, but then crashing back into my depression after work or that day's activities. But when I was ready to explore it, I started asking deeper questions. These questions, when explored, can bring you answers for yourself. These answers will help you move through the depression.

As I did this exploration, I realized there were a lot of things I didn't like about myself and my life. I realized I had a lot of anger, resentment, and sadness in me. I focused a lot on processing the pain and emotions I uncovered.

Psychedelic medicine helped me immensely. This medicine creates a safe blanket of love to explore deep wounded places inside you that you might be too scared to explore. I am a huge advocate of this medicine and now work as a life coach in psychedelic therapy in the mental health industry. I have seen hundreds of clients and have seen immense transformations for people with depression, anxiety, and more.

As I processed the pain inside me and made new discoveries, I made changes in my life with those insights. For example, I noticed I would feel more depressed around certain people, places, or situations. I would take note of this, explore why, and also limit my time and interactions with these spaces. All the small changes made a huge difference.

Does depression go away completely? I'm not sure. I think everyone has their own unique journey. I have definitely had lots of ups and downs, but I have found new ways to manage and work with them. I will say that I feel less depressed than I ever have. I find that the heavy depression I had has definitely lifted. So, something is working for sure!

Journal and Reflection Questions

1. How am I feeling right now? Why?
2. What are the feelings specifically that I feel?
3. Do I feel depressed?
4. From 1-10, where am I, with 10 being very depressed?
5. Why do I feel depressed?
6. What's sitting heavy in my heart right now?
7. What am I upset about?
8. What am I worried about?
9. What do I wish were different?

10. What do I really need right now?

11. What will fill up my cup?

12. How can I care for myself?

13. What's one small thing I can do for myself?

14. What's one thing you like about yourself?

15. What's one thing I'm proud of?

16. What's one thing I forgive myself for?

Anxiety

Sometimes I get super anxious when I'm driving. One thing that has helped me a ton is to focus on the road lines ahead of me. When I do that, I feel calmer, like I can do this. I tested this tip in other areas of my life and found it helpful. If I am anxious at an event, I'll find one thing to focus my attention on.

Emotional Freedom Technique (EFT) is also super helpful for in the moment anxiety and long-term anxiety you might be working through. It also helps with working through the pain of traumatic events because you are tapping on meridian points on your body. A teacher I recommend is Nick Ortner, the author of *The Tapping Solution*.[9]

Medicine is also helpful with anxiety. When I went through a psychedelic therapy program, I noticed that there were certain events that would usually send me over the edge. Psychedelic medicine helped me to distance myself from the event that was happening, and I noticed this bubble floating in my head, but I didn't get charged up, anxious, or upset. I was amazed by this. Many of my clients who have gone through this therapy have shared similar results with me. They found themselves less anxious in certain situations they would've normally been very anxious in.

Breathing is probably the best available technique. When you find yourself anxious, stop what you are doing and take a few deep breaths.

When I lead self-care circles, often the participants are just coming home, or getting off a work call, and are anxious and flustered. Once we do breathing exercises together, I can visibly see the calmness in everyone's face. My favorite technique is a simple 3-3-3 count. As I've mentioned, this is three counts pulling air in, holding for three counts, and releasing for three counts.

Another great tool is to create an Anxiety Log. My anxious clients love this activity. It brings them a lot of clarity as they notice patterns of what times of the day they were anxious, in what scenarios, and how they handled it.

Journal and Reflection Questions

1. How anxious do I feel on a scale of 1-10 (with 10 being very anxious)?
2. When do I feel anxious?
3. What events trigger the anxiety?
4. What does the anxiety feel like?
5. Where do I feel it in my body?
6. At what times of the day do I feel anxious?
7. What helps calm my anxiety down?
8. What are some ways I can make friends with the anxiety?
9. What is the anxiety trying to tell me?

Suicidal Ideation

If you are having thoughts of ending your life, or have had them before, first I want to say, "I love you." I know that we've never met, but I know this pain, and I know how isolating and difficult it can be. I'm writing this section for you.

You may not feel comfortable getting help or telling anyone the kind of thoughts going on in your head. You may feel shame. You may feel like a loser. You may feel like you can't get it together and wonder how other people are coping. You may think something is wrong with you. You may think you are a burden to others. You may feel other things I haven't listed here.

Here's what I want you to know: You are loved. And there is a loving path available to you.

It will require courage, willingness, and most importantly, honoring yourself (no matter what anyone has to say).

I never knew the level of depression I was in until it hit me and knocked me down. It started from a heartbreak and dwindled into so much deep pain. It was extremely hard to face, and I had so much shame around it. I wondered why I couldn't just get over it, or be grateful and like my life, like the other people around me.

Working with a Shaman helped me immensely. She was witness to my pain, held space for me to share my true thoughts, even the scary ones, she made me feel safe to explore my deeper thoughts.

Our culture is fixated on convincing people that ending your life is wrong, but there's not enough help in discovering what is causing the depression and navigating and healing it. So, here's what I want to offer you. I want you to explore your ideation deeper. This involves exploring how you form your ideas. Ask questions .First create a safe, nurturing, and nonjudgmental space for yourself before you start answering.

It also might be helpful to go deeper with a witness, a friend, a mentor, a therapist, a shaman, a coach, or someone else you trust.

Journal and Reflection Questions
1. What am I feeling right now?
2. Why do I feel this way?
3. What is causing me to feel this way?
4. In a perfect world, what would make this better?
5. What would make me happy?
6. What do I want?

7. What do I desire?
8. How do I want to live?
9. How can I feel better about myself?
10. What sensations do I feel in my body?
11. If no one was watching, what is the life I would live?
12. How can I honor my pain right now?
13. How can I nurture myself?

Depression is a call
For the Discovery of the self
Of the inside
Of the layers of pain
Waiting to be uncovered
Released
Freed
Discovered
ADITI RAMCHANDANI

CHAPTER **11**

Forming Habits for
Long-Term Gains

I fear not the man who has practiced 10,000 kicks,
but I do fear the man who has practiced one kick 10,000 times.
BRUCE LEE

Have you ever tried to build a habit in twenty-one days? Did it work? I don't know about you, but I've tried to do this, and let me tell you, there was usually no new habit to be found at the end of that month. In this chapter, I'll share with you why people struggle building habits, and what has worked for me to build new habits, and what I have seen work with clients and peers.

Why People Struggle When Building Habits

There are so many books on building habits, yet many people struggle with this. I believe there are a few reasons why. Before we dive into what works, let's talk about the struggles so we can address them up front.

Ninety-five percent of the body runs on subconscious programs. Our brains and bodies like routine and habit. Joe Dispenza, neuroscientist and author, explains in a documentary called *Rewired*[10] that by age thirty-

171

five, our blueprint program of life is built. We do the same things, we think the same things, and create a lot of the same recurring results. So, in order to go against this program, we only have 5 percent of our conscious brain working against 95 percent of our automatic subconscious. This is the number-one reason it is so hard to change and create a new habit. The good news is there are ways to change, but it will require a bit more effort. And more of that is mental effort than physical effort!

Check out Joe Dispenza's books to learn more about how to create change in your life and do the "Supernatural," as he calls it. His work has helped me immensely, and specifically this concept helped me realize why I struggled so much in creating change. It takes willingness, patience, and perseverance to become a new person and reprogram yourself. Here's what I'll tell you from doing the work, even though it sucked sometimes, it's SO worth it. And these changes you make slowly end up lasting longer in your life rather than just a six-week experiment (which are good too).

We live in an instant gratification culture. We have been sold this idea of fast results and the on-the-go solutions with the marketing messages that we are constantly inundated with at home on TV, on the road, and really anywhere we go—five-minute instant noodles, lose ten pounds in ten days, and so on. We have become obsessed with having fast results with little to no work. Anyone who has gone through a weight-loss journey or achieved any big goal knows that results take time and work.

The Non-Glamorous Process

When we are already tired from work and life, building a new habit that requires work is not very enticing, especially if it feels like a chore. Writing this book sounded like an awesome idea, but actually doing the work wasn't always fun. This doesn't mean it has to be an entirely miserable process, but there must be other factors driving you forward. It can't be simply because it sounds like a nice idea.

It makes sense why so many people have had big ideas or goals but have never achieved them. It requires all of you, a fully embodied approach. Achieving big goals is not for the dabblers. It's for the committed and passionate. And that can be created and found within you.

This doesn't mean there is no glamour. It's just not what we expected. So where does the glamour live? In the person you become and the results you create because of your dedication. Each chapter I write I am blown away by myself, as I experience a new level of growth and am closer to a published book! There is so much magic I experience in that.

Fear of Rejection

Building new habits often means doing things differently than those around you. This means standing out, which can be a really difficult experience for some. Wanting to fit in is a survival instinct, because in the past community-based-living we were in, if you were not going along with the crowd, you were kicked out both literally and figuratively. It literally meant death. Now we live in a more independent society, but we are still living from these old dynamics.

Therefore, building a strong inner core is so important in creating these changes in your life. Your inner core, commitment, and desire has to be so much bigger than all the noise around you. Your commitment to yourself has to be bigger than the opinions of others. It will not always be an easy process, and might include some tears, frustration, and feelings of wanting to give up.

But know this: becoming a person with a strong foundation of self is the greatest gift you will ever give yourself. Becoming the best version of you trumps the suffering you may experience through the process. Being at home within yourself feels like a million bucks.

Resistance

Our brain thinks 70,000 thoughts a day, and 90 percent are the same as yesterday, and the day before that. For the last decade! You've been thinking the same thoughts and living in the same patterns for decades. So of course there will be resistance to the unfamiliar. There can be a lot of resistance when starting something new.

Our brain likes familiarity. Our brain sticks to shortcuts. So, when it comes to creating a new habit, it's a long route for the brain, and it doesn't like it. Becoming familiar with the resistance and building a relationship with it can be powerful to help you move through it, and not let it stop you.

Cognitive Dissonance

It can be difficult to be in two places at once—being someone who doesn't practice self-care, but also becoming someone who does. This can cause confusion and friction in the brain. It doesn't know who or what is real and wants to go back to the old way of being. Being able to be in this discomfort of two worlds is what will allow you to experience change and growth.

Disconnected from Your Why

Your reason for building a new habit has to be deeply connected to your values, core, and desires. If you don't have a compelling reason to do this, it will easily become a forgotten chore at the end of your list. You also cannot be doing this because you think you "should" or because someone told you to. It has to truly come from within, from your own heart. How can you create a heart-connected why? Refer to the Part One: Foundations for more on this.

How to Build Habits

Most of us pick a new habit and just try to do it starting tomorrow with no other preparation work. I have found that building habits takes building a foundation for it to actually last. It requires physical, mental, and emotional preparation and continual nurturing.

One of the best ways that has helped me create new habits every time I am starting from scratch is to remind myself of the three phases of building habits. Knowing these three phases will help you navigate the experience.

Three Phases of Building Habits

Phase 1: Kickoff—This May Feel Like an Uphill Battle

I find that the first phase is often the hardest because it's doing something new. It might feel hard and uncomfortable initially, but it gets easier over time. The first week or two you may have a "starter high" of excitement, but that often wears off and you need something else to sustain you.

What will keep you going before the habit is built is your reasons for why you're doing this and your commitment to it. Remind yourself that it will get easier, and we just gotta cross this "river of misery" as my coach calls it.

When I did my very first stress management talk, it was the hardest thing I had ever done. I had many panic attacks, meltdowns, and constant freakouts about doing it. After I did my first one, I was like *WOW, I did it.* After I did my second one, I thought, *Okay, I think I can do this.* By the time I got to the third talk, it was SO much easier that it blew my mind.

Phase 2: Game Time—You Are in It

By now you might be realizing how much better you're feeling and wondering why you weren't doing this all along. The work might not always be fun, but the rewards are often worth it. You are starting to reap the benefits.

In the middle of any new habit creation, there will definitely be days you'll still want to give up and cry, but it will be so much easier to keep it up than it was to start. Reflecting on how far you've come since the beginning can be a huge confidence booster. Reconnecting to your why and commitment will keep you going.

Phase 3: Beyond—The Finish Line and What Comes Next

This is probably the easiest stage, but sometimes it can be very hard because you're so close to the finish line that you want to quit. You will still face some hard days where you won't want to do it, but you'll be so glad you did. This is crossing the finish line of what you committed to and continuing beyond that. Whether you committed to a ten-day or a 100-day self-care challenge, completion is a huge win, and then there is what happens after that.

Most importantly, this process isn't linear. You will have all kinds of emotions and life things come up through the process, but your commitment through this process will serve you well. Allow yourself to be open and flexible with the process, rather than getting mad about it not going your way or wishing it would be easier.

Helpful Tools to Build Habits

Creating Incentives

Rewards can be helpful in your journey to have something to look forward to. You should not rely on these incentives to motivate you because that may or may not work. But this is one way to add some fun to the process. See what works for you, and if you're not sure, try it! If you do decide to have incentives, make sure to follow through on what you decided. For example: if you promised yourself a new book at the end of your personal self-care ten-day challenge, don't give it to yourself until you have completed it.

When I did the ninety-day Hot Yoga challenge, I gave myself a book when I completed it. I had gotten the gift early and wrapped it, but I didn't let myself open it until I crossed the finish line. I can't say I wasn't tempted to just screw it and open my gift, but holding on to gift it to myself made it all the sweeter when I finally got it.

Tracking Your Progress

Keeping account of your progress is very helpful to allow you to see how you are doing, notice patterns of where you are struggling, and create pivots to try new ways. This could mean writing everything in a journal, having a calendar, or tracking it in an app.

A handful of my clients love to print out a giant physical calendar and track their progress visually there. If you like stickers, you can use those for each day when you complete your action. Another fun one that I got from my coach was having a clear jar that you fill with marbles. Each time you complete a day, you add a marble to a jar. There is a level of satisfaction our brain gets from seeing progress, and the marbles are a fun way to do that. Once your jar is filled to a certain point, that could be a time to reap your incentive that you created for yourself!

How to Have Long-Lasting Change

Swap Instant Gratification for Long-Term Gains

This will be a mindset shift you will do repeatedly. Because our brains have been conditioned to want quick results, we have to redirect our brain to a new place. Remind our brain that we are in this for the long-term gain, rather than the instant gratification.

And because your brain likes instant gratification, we can give it that too, but just in a new way. This is where the tracking/incentives can be helpful. Your instant gratification could be dropping a new marble into the jar. It's a cool way to gain both the long and short term gratification.

For example, if you are starting a daily walking routine, you may think it takes months to gain results, but the truth is, you get an instant gratification from the walk that day. You might have a clearer head, feel lighter, or simply calmer from walking it out that day.

Patience, Gratitude, and Compassion

These three can be super helpful through the journey. Think about how you can have *patience* with yourself. One of my favorite ways to do this is to come into the present moment. It can be so easy to focus on what you don't have, but when we can spend even just a little bit of time delighting in what we do have this can shift your energy completely.

Gratitude is an overused word that sometimes we are tired of hearing as advice. But the truth is it works when you are able to connect to it. One of my favorite exercises is to write down everything you want that you already have. Often when we get something we wanted, the excitement wears off after two weeks, and then we move on to wanting something else. But now we can have gratitude for all the things we have that we have wanted. What a beautiful thing.

Compassion is the most helpful and healing of all. When you are struggling on this journey, always turn to compassion. How can you have compassion for your struggle? Your pain? Your anger?

There are two things that have been super helpful in the journey that I want to share with you:

Pomodoro Method

This is my favorite habit hack, which I lovingly call the "tomato method" because it's easier to say. This hack also helps with productivity. The method is setting a twenty-five-minute timer and doing focused work with no distractions. That means turning off any phone notifications, social media, and putting a pause on checking mail. Then you take a five-minute break to do whatever you'd like. Then you can start another twenty-five-minute timer if you'd like.

When I haven't wanted to clean or write, I always use this hack to help me. I believe you can do anything for twenty-five minutes. It doesn't seem overwhelming to the brain at all and makes it much more doable. You can use a timer on your phone, on Google (there's a free one if you Google twenty-five minute timer), or you can buy a non-digital timer in the shape of an apple that you'll sometimes see on a teacher's desk.

In fact, I've used this method to write a lot of this book! It helped me feel less overwhelmed. And it was a small enough amount of time that I could commit to. Use this anytime you don't want to do something but would like to get it done or for more efficiency and focus.

Cue Trigger

This is attaching a new habit to something you already do. The thing you already do is a trigger and cues you to do the next thing. For example, my trigger to do oil-pulling (a technique to freshen and clean bacteria in your mouth) is brushing my teeth. So, before I brush my teeth, I always remember that I have to oil-pull first. This ensures I don't forget because it's the thing I do right before brushing my teeth always. It can also be helpful to have a visual trigger. For example: having the coconut oil jar ready for me in the bathroom so I don't forget before brushing my teeth.

My hope is that this chapter has made the idea of building a habit a little more doable and less daunting. Also addressing what may be stopping you from building a habit can be super helpful in identifying where you may be stuck.

In the next chapter we are going to take everything from this book and create a dedicated 100-day Self-Care Road Map for you. Use the tips in this chapter to help you execute your Self-Care Road Map.

CHAPTER 12

Your 100-Day Self-Care Road Map

It always seems impossible until its done.
NELSON MANDELA

The moment has come where we bring it all home. We've gone through a whole journey together, and now it's time to spring it to life on a whole new level. This chapter will be your take-home project after the completion of this book. If we were working together, this would be the assignment we'd craft together for you to launch into your journey.

With everything you've learned till now, we are going to take all that knowledge and put it into practice. This road map will serve you well as you start your journey, but it will also be the perfect thing to come back to anytime you want to refresh, restart, or redirect your self-care journey.

There are two main things to remember—no self-care plan is created equal, and there's no wrong way to do this! You can absolutely get ideas and inspiration from others, but don't rely on this because your needs are different from theirs. Your plan will be unique to you. You may find yourself wondering, *Am I doing this right?* There is no wrong or right way to do this besides what feels right for you.

If this process feels daunting or overwhelming to you, I want you to think about it as less of a chore, obligation, or another thing to add to your to-do list, but rather as a gift you are giving yourself—the gift of self-care. Who doesn't like gifts, right?

In this chapter I will give you options so you can custom create your own path, but I will also give a recommended road map for those who like to be given a step-by-step approach to follow. Over time you will find what works for you and tweak it as you need to. Now let's create your road map!

Creating Your Road Map

1. Pick a Time Container

The first step to creating your road map is picking a container of time to execute your road map. This chapter introduces the 100-Day Road Map, but I'm giving you the power to decide how many days your personal road map will be.

The reason we pick a time frame and not "forever" is that forever feels daunting and overwhelming for most people, and an easy reason to not start at all. So instead, we are going to start with a chunk of time to focus on and then, after you complete that, you can decide your next steps. From there you can decide what you want to "keep forever" or tweak to match your schedule and needs. This saves your mind from feeling trapped or locked in forever—especially when it's something new and possibly unfamiliar!

Doing something in repetition helps it become more of an ingrained habit. When you do something good for your body, it will naturally crave more of it. It's almost like this focused time is creating that trigger or craving in your body for more. This is a good thing!

Have you ever eaten really clean for a few weeks or months and then ate some heavy processed foods and afterward CRAVED a salad? It's similar to that! Once your body gets a taste of some goodness that replenishes it, it asks for more!

So how much time will your focused container of self-care be? Do you want to do a short-term container or a long-term container? Depending on where you are in your journey, if you are a self-care beginner or advanced, you can decide what is realistic for you and what you know you can commit to. Some people are ready to jump in for the long haul, and others are comfortable jumping into a challenge for a shorter time period. Do whatever works for you, but most importantly ,do something.

A short-term container could be ten or thirty days. A longer-term container could be one hundred days or one full year. If you're not sure where to start, my recommendation is always one hundred days. It's a good amount of time to root a new habit in you, but it's also not painstakingly long and has a finite end so you don't feel trapped for life. You want to get to a point where you actually desire to do these habits versus feeling like it's part of a plan.

After you've decided your container, then it's time to decide when you'll start and end. For example, if you choose one hundred days, you can google "100 days from now" or "100 days from x date" to see what date it would end. Then go ahead and write it down in this book or in your self-care journal.

My personal Self-Care Road Map will be for _____ days and starts on this date _____ and ends on this date

_____.

2. Decide Your Activity

Next decide what you will do within this container of time. My recommendation is to commit to one self-care activity. If you are not a beginner and want to commit to more than one activity, I recommend picking one main commitment with up to four more add-on activities.

Decide on the activity, how long you will do it for, and at what point in the day you'll do it. I find that picking a time of the day and sticking to it makes it easier to accomplish and helps keep you accountable.

Also note that I use the word *activity*, but we know that self-care isn't always about "doing" as we spoke about earlier. But in this case, activity could mean being present, or being kind, or something that has to do with who you are being versus an actual physical activity. Allow yourself to get creative with this. Use the answers from Chapter 5: Recharge to give you ideas for different activities.

Think about an area of your life that you are feeling called to care for more. It might be many areas, and that's okay too. Pick one that feels the most important and relevant. And if you are not sure, just make a decision and pick one. Remember, there's no right or wrong; there's simply showing up and caring for yourself that matters, no matter what it looks like.

How Long Will You Do Your Activity For?

Many of my clients want to jump to thirty or sixty minutes for their activity, and those are great times. But when I ask them what a realistic time is that they can commit to, often they lessen the amount. When I give them permission to choose five minutes if that's something they can truly commit to, some of them are so relieved because that feels super doable for them and they were getting stressed out thinking about a longer time frame.

Choose what feels good for you and what you know you can realistically commit to. Some of my clients were able to easily commit to a thirty to ninety-minute activity, but most of my clients choose something that takes five to fifteen minutes. Again, there is no right or wrong on what you choose. I will repeat that a million times in this book because everyone always forgets that!

Notice your thoughts about the time you choose as well. Do you think of yourself less because you chose a smaller time? Think about how you can encourage yourself for what you chose instead of belittling yourself—that's where the compassion comes in handy.

When Will You Do Your Activity?

If you're someone who is wholeheartedly against doing your activity at a certain time every day, I have a couple of other options for you.

An alternate option is to pick a completion time. This means that by a certain time each day you are committed to having completed that activity. My clients LOVE when I propose this idea to them. It gives them the freedom and flexibility to do their activity at a time that feels right for them.

For example, Let's say you committed to meditating every day for ten minutes and you selected a completion time for 6:00 p.m. This means that every day your meditation will have been completed by 6:00 p.m. You can choose a check-in time, whether that's in the middle of the day or at 5:00 p.m. At that time, you check in to see when you'll complete it, and if you haven't already, then the time is now.

Another alternate option is to have a cue set up. For instance, "Whenever I grab the mail in the morning, that's when I will practice self-compassion toward myself." So you attach the activity to another activity you already do in your life. This works great, too, for some of my clients. Try whichever method works for you. And if you're not sure, test one out on week one and another on week two.

3. Start Your Journey

This is the most important step. A lot of people do all the planning work, but never get to actually doing the journey. Not you. We are going to prepare you, so you have what you need to get started.

Scheduling

First, let's talk about scheduling. I would plug this into a calendar that you use often. For example: if you decide you want to take fifteen-minute breaks every three hours, you can schedule that into your calendar. Or if you plan to go for a daily workout at 10:00 a.m., schedule that into your calendar as well.

The kicker of this road map is that if you miss a day, you must start from day one again. This is one of the best incentives to not forget or skip! Remember you may face resistance, and that is completely normal. Allow yourself to feel the resistance and show up for yourself through nurturing and hearing yourself out. Sometimes I have to reason with myself or make promises and incentives to get me into action.

Tracking and Accountability

Now let's discuss tracking. Just because you scheduled it doesn't mean it always happens, right? So, we must track how we are showing up to our self-care appointments. There are different ways you can track to be accountable to yourself, so feel free to get creative with this. Some of my clients like to print out or buy a big calendar they can post on their wall and mark Xs, or they place stickers or stars on each day they did their self-care activity. Some track it in a journal or in an app. What would work best for you? And most importantly, what would be FUN for you?

Another helpful way to be accountable is to have an accountability buddy! Know someone who wants to do a challenge together? Ask them to join you! Grab a self-care partner, give them a copy of this book, create your self-care plans together, and execute together! Have a check-in once a week to tell each other how it's going and to lift each other up!

Rewards

Is there something that would be enticing for you that would make your self-care appointment more important to complete for you? I'll be honest, I did not want to write today. But I committed to writing at least twenty-five-minutes a day to finish this book after taking a three-month hiatus. Because I could see my resistance, I asked myself what a nice reward would be after finishing. My answer? *Bridgerton, Season Two.*

As soon as I finish writing today, I am going to get cozy and watch my current favorite Netflix show. What's even more amazing is that I committed to only twenty-five minutes, but I got so in the zone that now it's been over sixty minutes that I've been writing.

So, notice for yourself what reward would make it more exciting for you to complete your self-care activity each day. It could be different rewards or the same thing each day. Maybe once you finish, you get to have a delicious smoothie or cuddle with your pup!

Meet yourself where you are and hold your hand through the process. Sometimes it takes nurturing, sweet talk, and reminding yourself of your bigger reason to get moving, especially on those hard days when you don't want to do anything. You got this!

Executing Your Road Map

Plan for Perfection and Allow for Redirection

It's time to bring your road map to life! This is the part where we truly step into our commitment and practice of self-care and filling our cups. One thing I want to note is that the idea of filling up our cup sounds like roses and daisies, but there are many times it doesn't feel so good. Self-care can often feel like a detox as well.

When you are constantly ON and decide to stop, it can feel terrible. And the idea of self-care no longer feels so nice. But here's what I want you to know—it eventually DOES FEEL GOOD. Maybe not in the moment, maybe not even right after, but over time you are going to feel better. It's like depositing small checks into your bank account. It doesn't seem like a lot and might not satisfy you, but over time it sure will add up. It's the same thing with self-care. It adds up.

When I started the 75 HARD challenge, the first week was fun and exciting, but soon it became crippling. My body was in so much pain from all the working out I was doing that sometimes I was in tears as I was going to bed because my body was aching so much. It felt miserable and horrible, but there were parts that felt nice too—even rejuvenated. The opportunity to go outside and clear my head in the middle of the day for forty-five minutes became my medicine.

There was even a period during that seventy-five days where my plantar fasciitis really flared up. That was probably the roughest part of the challenge. My feet were in pain, but I had committed to this challenge, and I wanted to make it work, so I made the workouts lighter and more stretching/yoga-focused. Once I moved through that hump, my feet were fine again, and it's almost like I never had plantar fasciitis. Of course, you want to be gentle and consult with a doctor when necessary, but over time you will learn how to work with your body through the journey.

Even though there were awful parts of the journey, overall I felt much better. And now outdoor walking has become a regular part of my self-care. It refreshes me, lightens me, and resets me. So, remember, even if it feels awful at first, it will feel better as time goes on. It's almost like you are repairing the broken holes in your cup before you can fill it up.

Motivating Yourself

I know a lot of you will be asking, "But how do I motivate myself?" There are a few things that will help you motivate yourself, which are listed below. My goal through this 100-day challenge is that after you complete it, you won't have to motivate yourself as much anymore.

At the time of writing this book, I am picking up my daily walking habit again, which I dropped for a month or two while traveling. It was so easy for me to pick back up. I was easily able to motivate myself for walking because I know now how much my mental and physical health benefits from it. It wasn't hard to convince myself to go walking every day for forty-five minutes. I wish I could bring this habit into my writing. Maybe soon!

The motivation I have to have for writing is still painful to some degree. It's almost like I drag myself to the computer. I realized part of the reason it's so hard for me is because of all the negative thoughts that are circling in my head about writing, my abilities, my worth, my concern of others' opinions, but most of all I don't want to face my OWN OPINION, which is often quite harsh. I'm learning to be kinder to myself for my writing efforts. You'll see below that one of my points for motivation is kinder self-talk.

Embodying That Commitment in Your Whole Being

For one, this is why you are going to do a 100-day challenge. It is not a question or an idea; it is a commitment you have made. Embodying it means feeling it in your spirit and showing up as a person who does self-care challenges.

Deeper Connection to Your Why

The most important thing to motivate yourself is to connect to your why. Why are you are doing this? What is self-care going to do for you? What will it allow you to do? Some of the work in the earlier chapters will help you dig deeper into discovering and getting clear on your why.

Kind Self-Talk

Notice for yourself what your self-talk is around doing this challenge. Are you berating yourself? Are you saying it's going to be too hard? I'll tell you, whatever you declare is what you will end up experiencing. Take notice of the words you are using to describe the things you want to do, and your ability to do them, because I promise that is affecting your motivation too.

See Yourself as What You Want to Become

What if you start to see yourself as someone who journals every day, or runs in their lunch breaks [fill in the blank of your self-care activity]? This is a profound shift that helps a lot. If you keep seeing yourself through the eyes of your old self, you'll likely keep doing the same thing. But if you start to see yourself differently, you will find yourself being that person more and more. It's just normal for me to go on forty-five-minute walks now. This wasn't the case before, and I didn't see myself as a walker. But now I do. And I started to see myself as a walker before I really became one! You are what you believe.

The Post-Road Map Journey

After you finish your journey, there are a couple things you can do. You can decide to take a break. Or you can decide to continue with the same routine. You might also decide to do a hybrid model, such as reducing it to three specific days a week versus doing it every day.

There have been times where I take a full break then come back to it in a week, and then decide how I want to incorporate this new habit into my life for the long term. There are other times when I just keep going with the new habit for a while longer, then decide on a long-term plan.

Remember that this isn't a linear journey. You might have some ups and downs along the way, but you can always find your way right back here. There are many times I found myself in a slump, and came back to starting a new 100-day self-care journey or some similar version of it.

You might have a habit that you built through your 100-day journey, but then find seven weeks later that you've skippped your routine. Remind yourself that this is okay. You don't want to fall too far off track, so try to give yourself a range that you'll check back in with yourself. But at the same time, if you do completely fall off track for months or even years, you can always pick right back up!

Most importantly, continue to encourage yourself rather than your naysayer voices taking center stage. Remember the 1 percent rule. Practicing even just 1 percent of self-care is phenomenal. Keep doing something, and remember that small tweaks can create great results over time.

My 100-Day Road Map Journey

I've done multiple journeys in my life, consisting of seven-day ones to 100-day ones. I have found the 100-day journeys to be the most effective for creating long-term habits, so that is what I believe in and include in my template.

As I was writing this book, I decided to do my own 100-Day Self-Care Road Map to test it out. It was around day thirty that I found myself stopping while I was traveling. I was bummed, but I decided I was going to honor the rules and start over. I realized that even if I had to start over, thirty days of walking was a huge win and gift to myself.

Each time, it feels a tiny bit less daunting for me because I have done 100-day journeys before. I noticed I was more at ease with it, but of course, not always! The first time you do this it will be quite a profound experience for you. It was for me when I did one hundred days of walking for the first time.

Because you develop a new level of intimacy with yourself, you will notice your excuses and the reasons you don't want to do it. You will notice your moods and befriend yourself through them. You will build a new level of friendship through this 100-Day Road Map, which is probably the most beautiful benefit you will get from doing this fully!

This is more than just self-care. It's truly an inside out, transformative experience with yourself. It is shifting your relationship with self-care and stress, shifting your relationship with yourself, and meeting a new version of yourself that you never knew existed.

Each 100-day journey I commit to changes me in some way. I hope that you will experience your own powerful truths through this journey. This is not a one-time thing, but rather something you can choose to do multiple times a year, or just once a year. It helps you refocus your energy and time toward what matters, your wellness. Now let's create your roadmap!

The 100-Day Road Map Template

Here is a plug-and-play template you can use as your baseline and modify it to work for you.

For Self-Care Beginners

1. Choose a 100-day container, a start date, and an end date.
2. Choose one nonnegotiable self-care activity you will gift yourself every day.
3. Decide how long you will spend doing it. I recommend a minimum of five to sixty minutes. Choose something realistic that is a no brainer and is doable for you.
4. Plan into your schedule the time of day or completion time.
5. Show up for your appointments with yourself and track your progress. If you miss a day, start over from day one.

For Self-Care Intermediate

1. Choose a 100-day container, a start date, and an end date.
2. Choose one nonnegotiable self-care activity you will gift yourself every day. Choose two to five more smaller things that you will add on week after week. Week two: add in activity two, week three add in activity three, etc.
3. Decide how long you will spend doing it. I recommend a minimum of twenty to sixty minutes. Choose something doable, but also make it a mini stretch to challenge you.
4. Plan into your schedule the time of day or completion time.
5. Show up for your appointments with yourself and track your progress. If you miss a day, start over from day one.

Sample 100-Day Road Map

1. 100-Day Self-Care Container is December 1 to March 11.
2. Twenty minutes of daily walking. Five minutes of meditation. Ten minutes of oil pulling. Say one kind thing to myself. Drink sixty ounces of water a day.
3. Walking completion time 10:00 p.m. Oil pulling right before brushing in the a.m. Everything else is completed by 6:00 p.m.
4. Plug into calendars. Create sticky note reminders on my desk. Set reminders on phone.
5. Show up and track in notes app in phone.

Remember, no road map will look the same. Some road maps will have more physical activities, while others will consist of more mental activities, and yet others will contain a mix of it all. It really depends on where you're at in your journey. Keep it simple, be kind to yourself, and start when you are ready.

What Happens after the 100 Days?

After the 100 days are over, first of all CELEBRATE! Because that's INCREDIBLE! Once you cross the finish line, you get to decide what you want to do next. Which habits do you want to keep in your life and continue with? And maybe which habits do you want to switch out to try something different?

From here you will create a self-care lifestyle. Decide what you want that to look like. Maybe you will continue what you did indefinitely. Or maybe you will tweak it a bit. Choose what works for you . . . but most importantly, renew your commitment to something sustainable for the long term.

After I finished my one hundred days of walking, I decided I wanted to continue walking whether it was daily or three to five times a week.

Walking has now become a big part of my life in a way that it never was before. It has become my new love. I love the way the crisp air feels on my skin. I love the way I am able to process emotions or difficult moments with a simple walk. I love taking walks with a neighbor or on a date.

When I find myself not having walked in a bit, my body starts to crave it. It makes me happy when I feel that because I know I have ingrained something in my body that makes her want more! If I find my self-care habits slipping, I'll often commit to a new challenge and create a new roadmap for myself. My current 100-Day Road Map consists of daily walking or movement for twenty minutes and oil-pulling. It makes me feel good to know I am showing up for myself.

Closing Thoughts

Stress can be a debilitating struggle in our life when we don't know how to work with it. My mission is to help you shift your relationship with stress so it no longer controls you, but rather gives you the information you need to navigate your life. Self-care will always lead you to your next step in life. When you are fully rested, cared for, and loved by yourself, you will have the space to hear your own inner whispers, and have the energy to follow them. Self-care is a lifelong journey, and you can use these tools forever.

Self-care has allowed me to experience a greater level of connection with myself, a deeper feeling of fulfillment and contentment that I've never felt before. I'm grateful to be able to share this information with you from my heart to yours.

If you have questions that come up that weren't addressed in the book, please send them to me as I continue to create more self-care materials to complement this book. At the back of this book, you will find a resources section with programs I've created for deeper study, along with books and videos I recommend.

You deserve all the happiness, success, and love that you desire. And it all starts with self-care. Caring for yourself allows you to tune into who you are, discover what your needs are, and cater to them. It has been a joy to spend this time together, and I hope this book has been a helpful guide on your self-care journey.

Sending you much love, and I hope we connect again.

Self-care has truly saved my life. And I'm excited to see how this journey unfolds for you.

HAPPY SELF-CARING!
Aditi Ramchandani

For more programs and deeper support visit:
www.aditicreative.com

References

1. Tosha Silver, *Outrageous Openness: Letting the Divine Take the Lead* (New York: Atria Books. 2014).

2. Louise Hay, *You Can Heal Your Body* (Carlsbad, CA: Hay House, 1985).

3. Glennan Doyle, *Untamed* (New Yori:The Dial Press, 2020).

4. Clinton Ober, Stephen T. Sinatra MD, Martin Zucker, *Earthing: The Most Important Health Discovery Ever!* (Laguna Beach, CA: Basic Health Publications, 2014).

5. Steve Hatfield, Jen Fisher, Paul H. Silvergate, "The C-Suite's Role in Well-Being," Deloitte Insights, June 22, 2022, https://www2.deloitte.com/us/en/insights/topics/leadership/employee-wellness-in-the-corporate-workplace.html?id=us2sm:3li4diUS175466:5awa::MMDDYY::author&pkid=1008950.

6. Milja, Milenkovic, *42 Worrying Workplace Stress Statistics. Daily Life Ezine*, September 25, 2019. https://www.stress.org/42-worrying-workplace-stress-statistics.

7. "Stress in America: The State of Our Nation," Stress in America Survey, 2017, American Psychological Association, http://www.apa.org/news/press/releases/stress/2017/state-nation.pdf.

8. "Research Proves Your Brain Needs Breaks," WTI Pulse Report, Microsoft Report; April 20, 2021, https://www.microsoft.com/en-us/worklab/work-trend-index/brain-research.

9. Nick Ortner, *The Tapping Solution: A Revolutionary System for Stress-Free Living* (Carlsbad, CA: Hay House, 2014).

10. Joe Dispenza, *Rewired,* Gaia.com, documentary series.

Resources and Next Steps

Resources: www.aditicreative.com/resources
This page includes a list of books, tools, and training videos to take your self-care journey further. I've also included articles I've published and holistic practitioners I recommend.

Programs: www.aditicreative.com/programs
Are you ready to take this book into practical action? Join the coaching program and online course I've created to compliment this book with audios and worksheets included. Want to learn and practice with me live? Come to my self-care retreats, writing programs, and live events that will be updated on this page.

Program inquiries: hello@aditicreative.com

Seminars: www.aditispeaks.com
Bring a self-care seminar to your community, team, organization, or friends gathering. I deliver virtual and in person talks and workshops. Contact our team to inquire. If you know someone who hires speakers, feel free to share my contact with them or connect us over email.

Speaking Inquiries: info@aditispeaks.com

Connect on Social Media: aditicreative.com/connect
Instagram@aditicreative